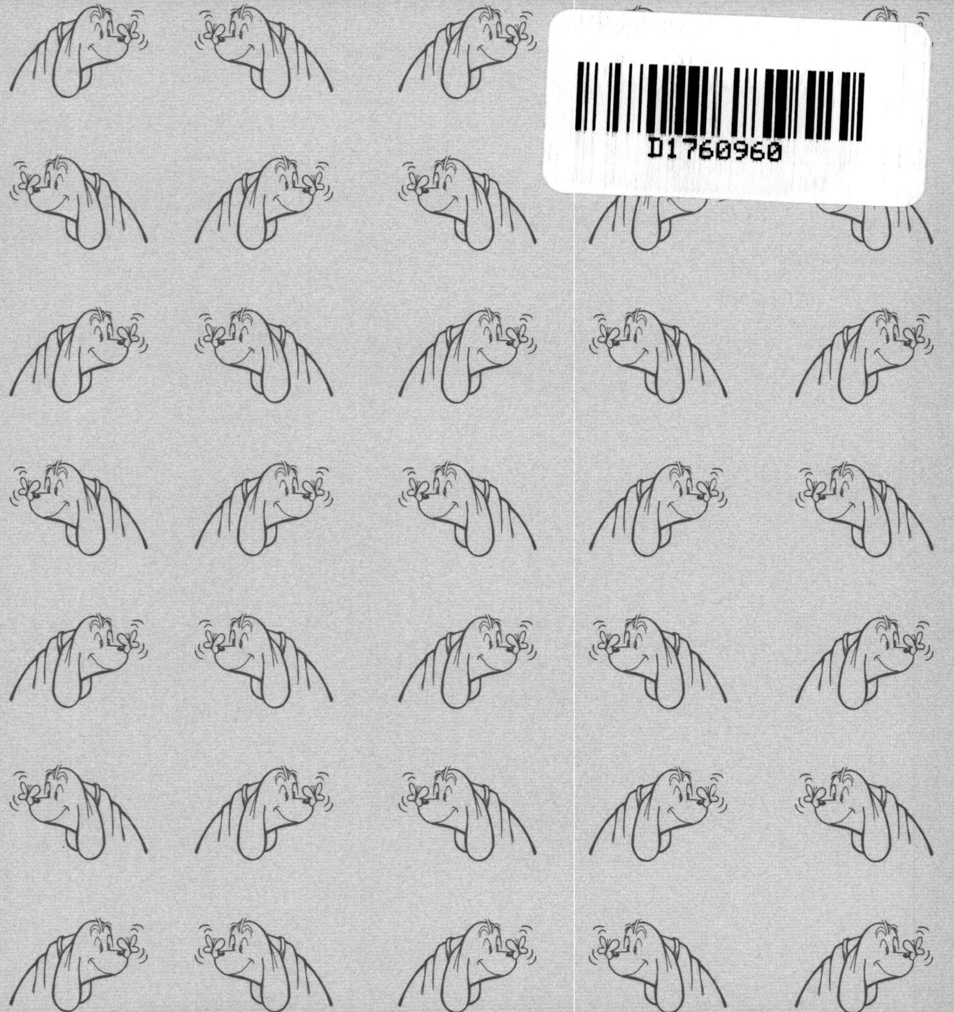

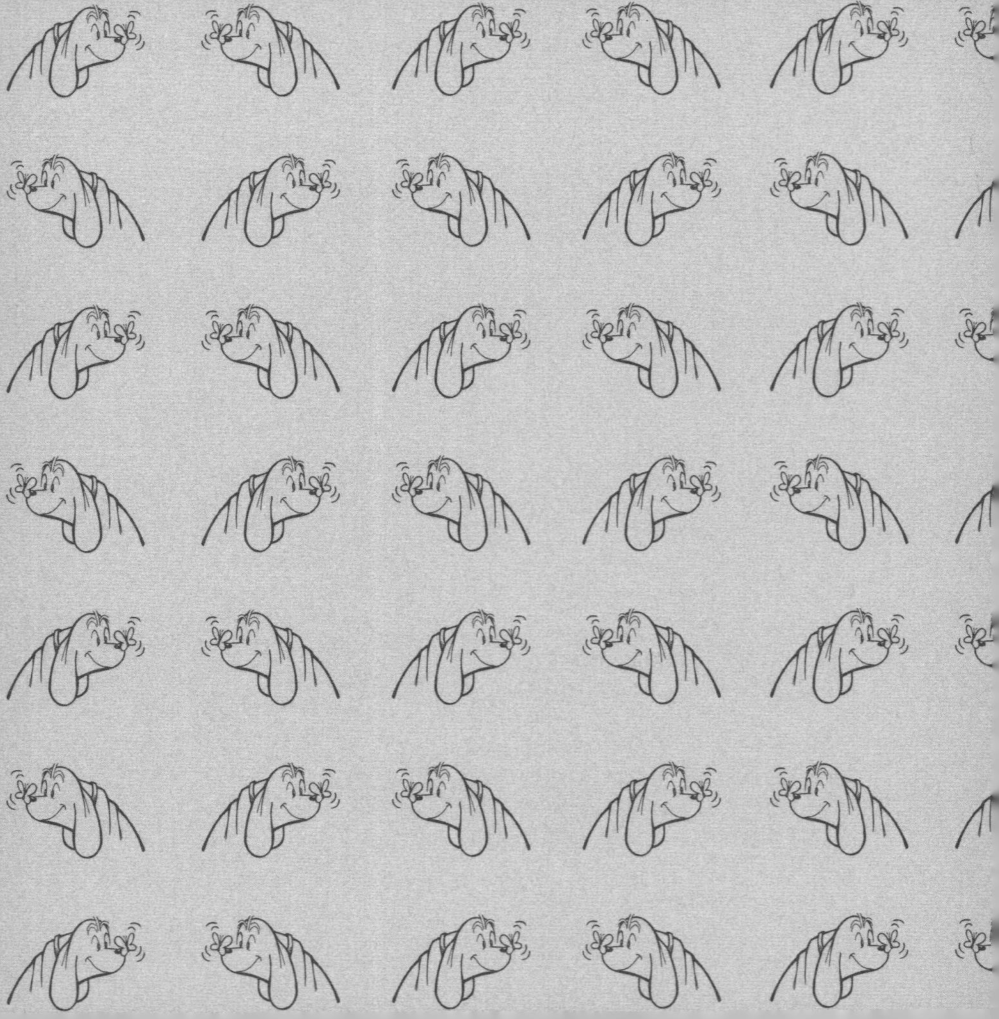

FRED BASSET

for Garden Lovers

summersdale

FRED BASSET FOR GARDEN LOVERS

Summersdale Publishers Ltd
46 West Street
Chichester
West Sussex
PO19 1RP
UK

www.summersdale.com

Printed and bound in China

ISBN: 978-1-84024-779-4
Drawings by Alex Graham and Michael Martin

Substantial discounts on bulk quantities of Summersdale books are available to corporations, professional associations and other organisations. For details telephone Summersdale Publishers on (+44-1243-771107), fax (+44-1243-786300) or email (nicky@summersdale.com).

FRED BASSET®

for Garden Lovers

Introducing Fred...

Fred Basset was created by Alex Graham in 1963, when he made his first appearance in the *Daily Mail*. He has held a regular spot in comic strips in the *Daily Mail* and *The Mail on Sunday* ever since. The popular pooch also features every year in calendars and has his very own annual, *The Fred Basset Yearbook*.

Fred Basset for Garden Lovers brings together the very best of Fred's garden moments over the years, in a collection of full colour images never before gathered together in book form.

Fred has always been in his element in the garden, whether he's finding the best sunbathing spot or helping with the garden chores.

He has plenty of adventures there too – there's next door's cat to chase off, and juicy bones to track down with his doggy pals, Jock and Yorky.

Of course, Fred gets into his fair share of mischief, when he roots out next year's daffodils or leaves muddy paw prints on the freshly cleaned kitchen floor.

But most of all, he reminds us that there aren't many places better to be than your own garden on a sunny day, and that a dog's life isn't such a bad life after all...

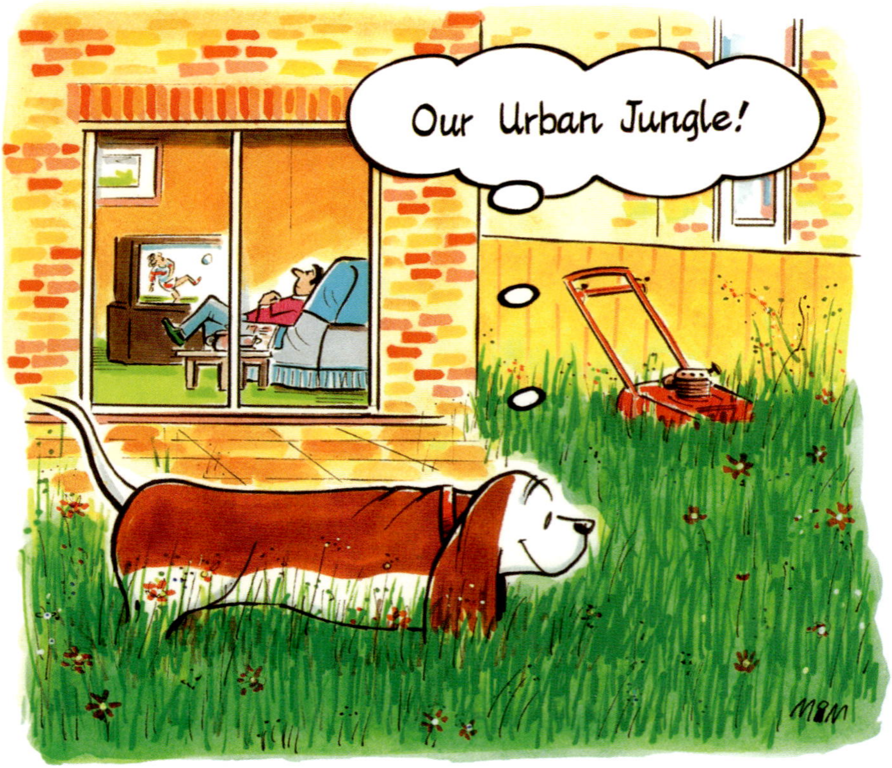
Our Urban Jungle!
MBM

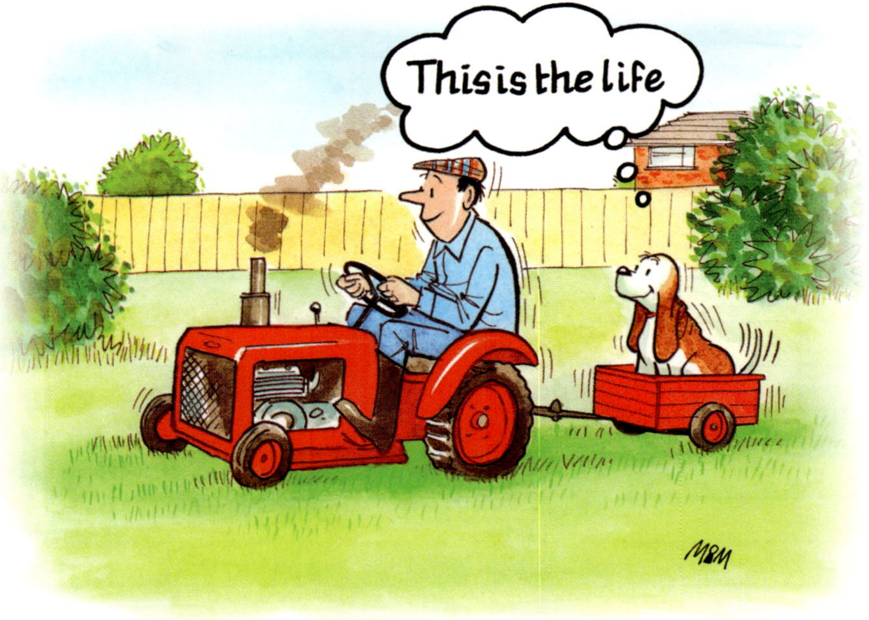
This is the life
M&M

I THINK FRED IS HAVING A FUNNY FIVE MINUTES!

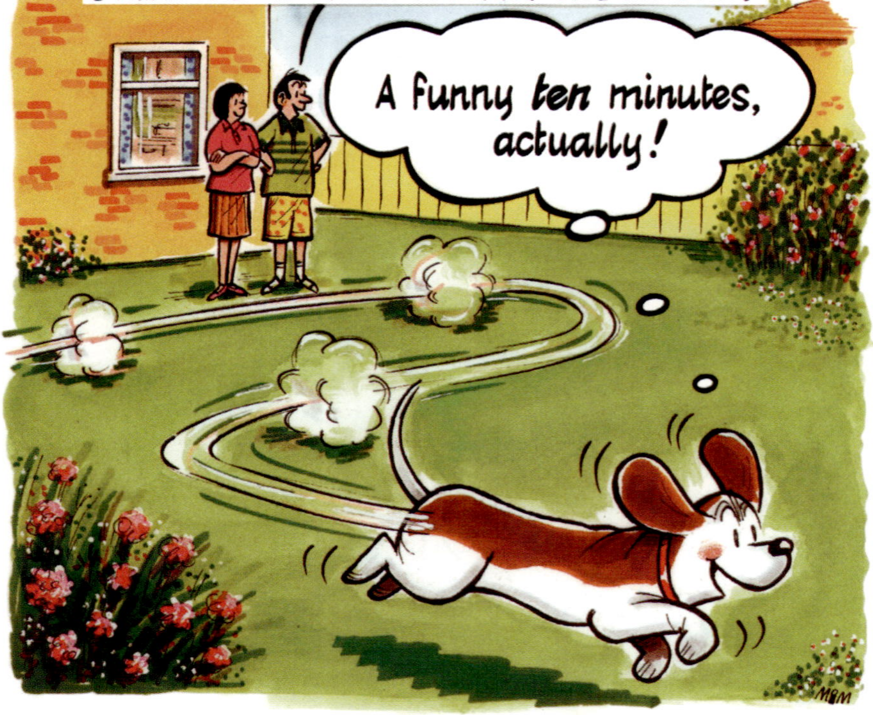
A funny *ten* minutes, actually!

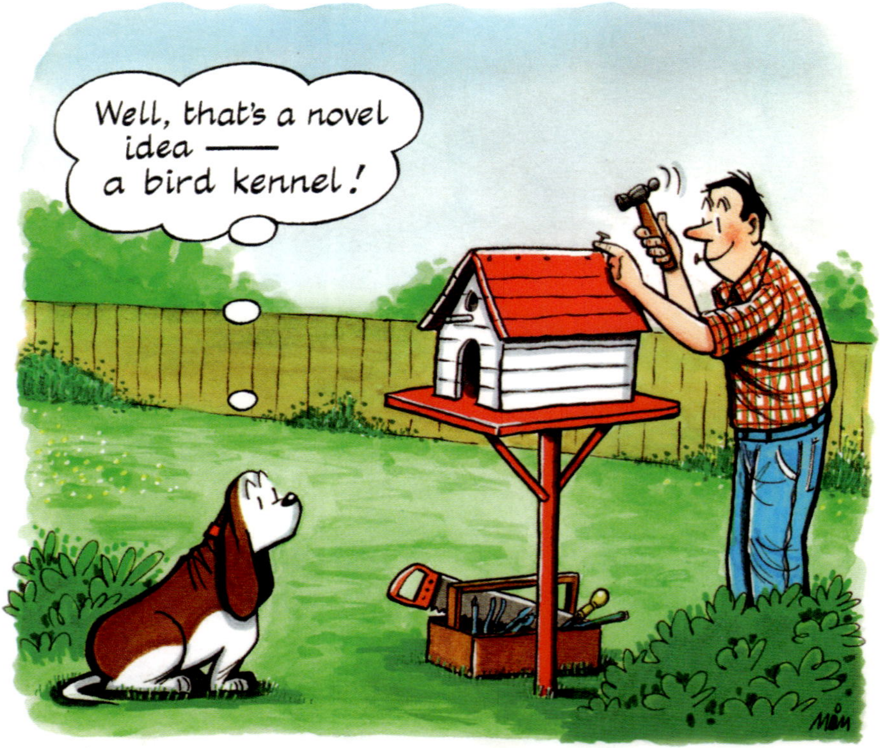
Well, that's a novel idea —— a bird kennel!

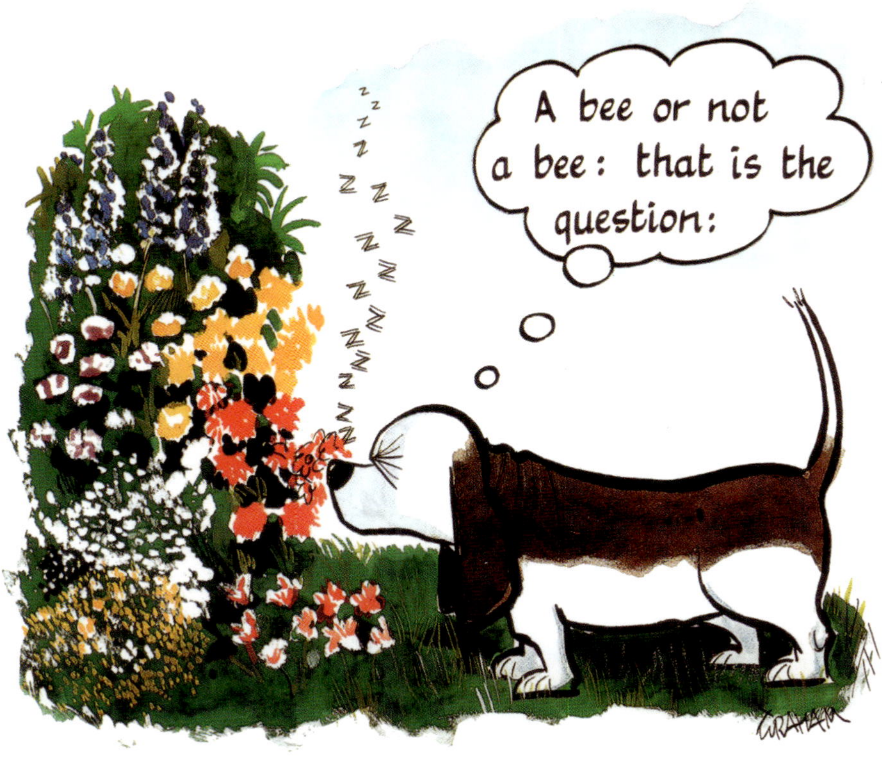
A bee or not a bee: that is the question:

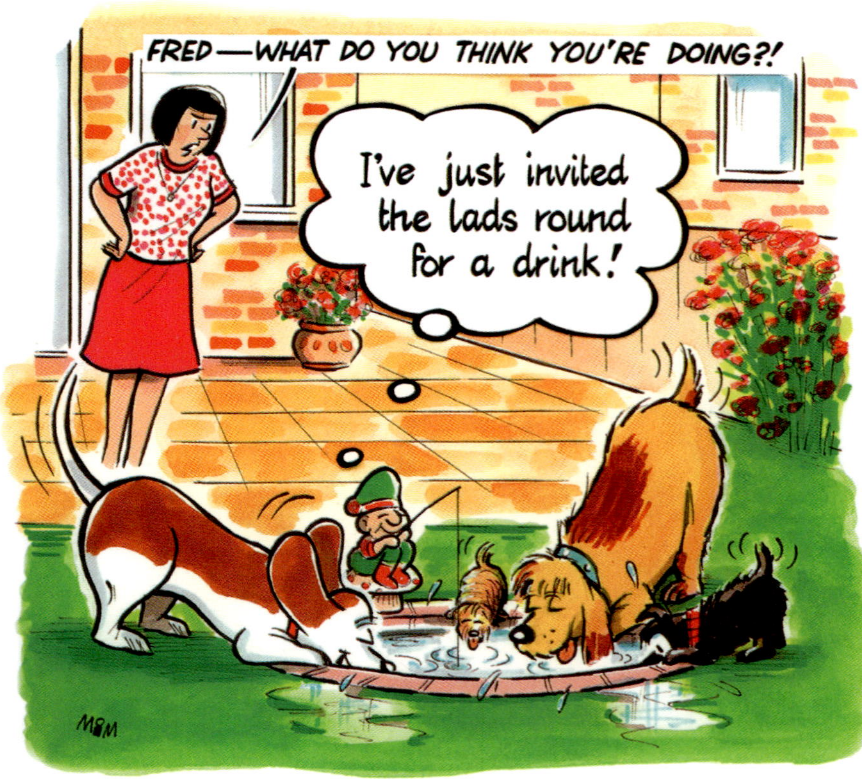
FRED—WHAT DO YOU THINK YOU'RE DOING?!
I've just invited the lads round for a drink!
M&M

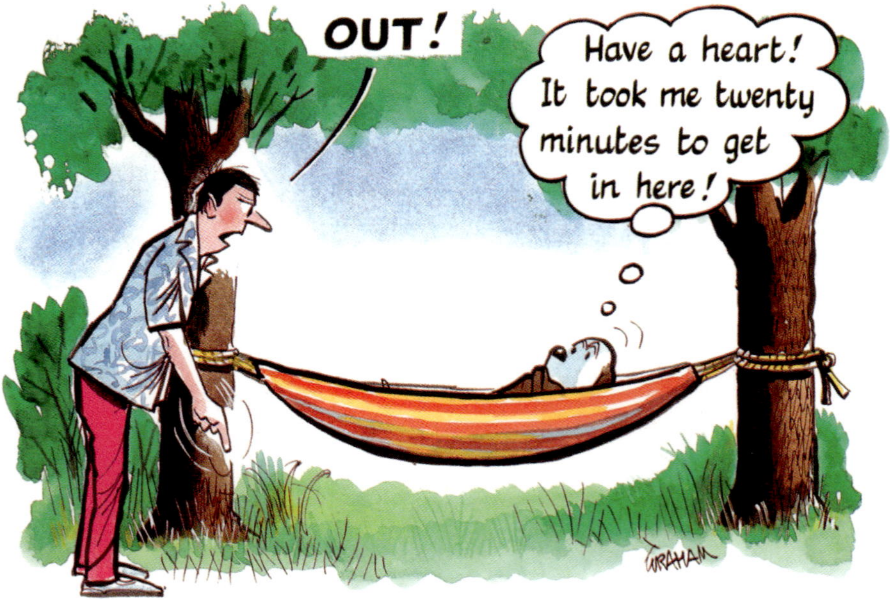

OUT!
Have a heart! It took me twenty minutes to get in here!
GRAHAM

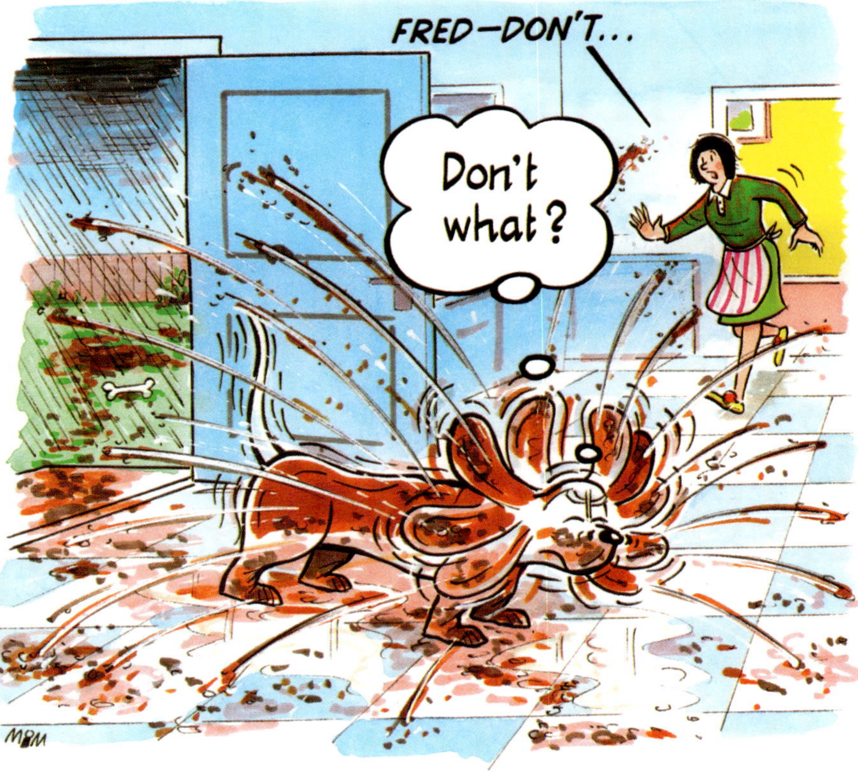
FRED—DON'T...
Don't what?
MGM

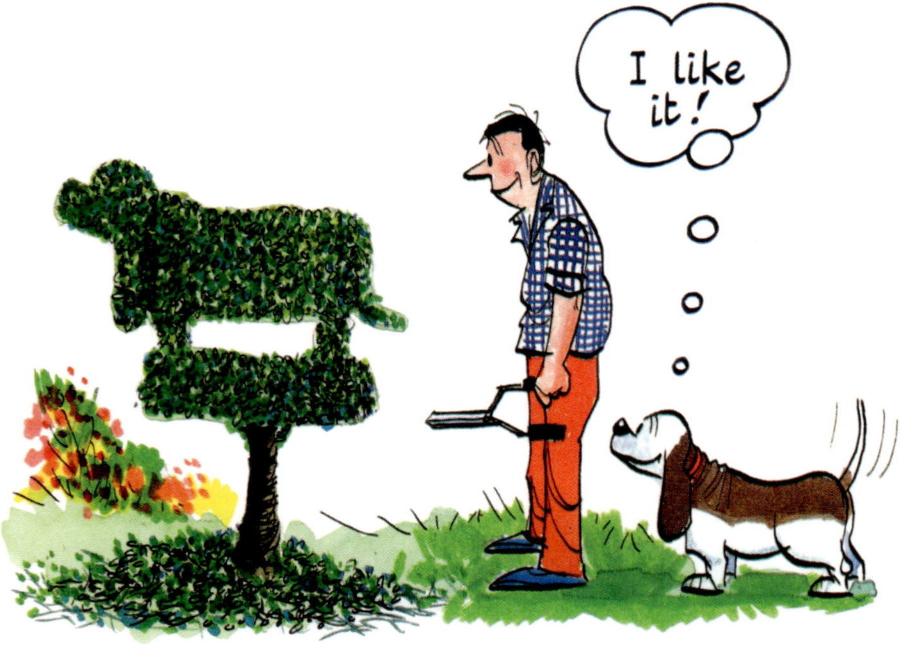
I like it!

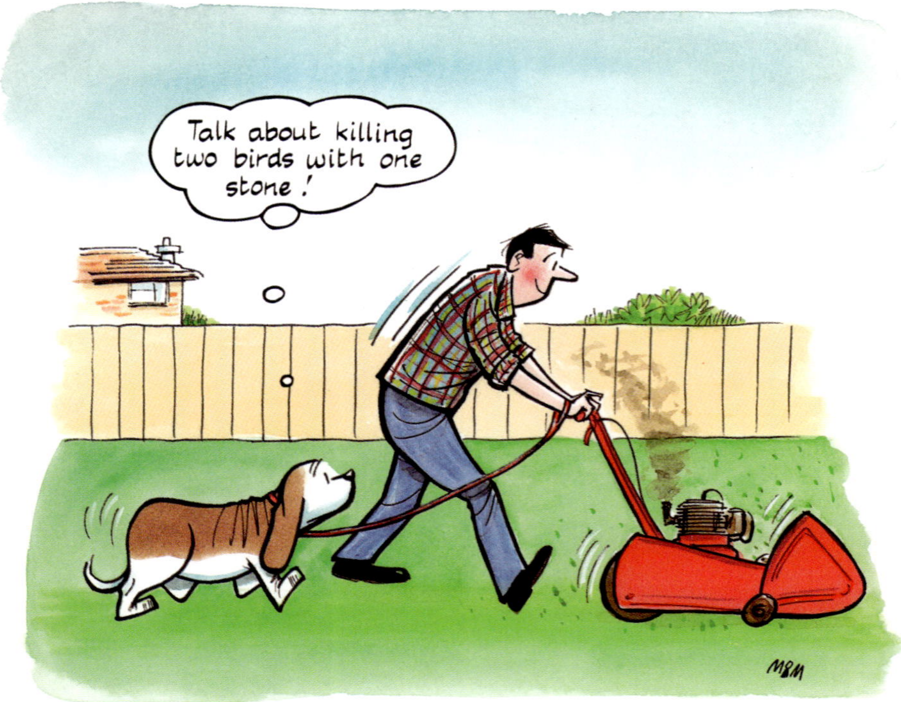
Talk about killing two birds with one stone!
M&M

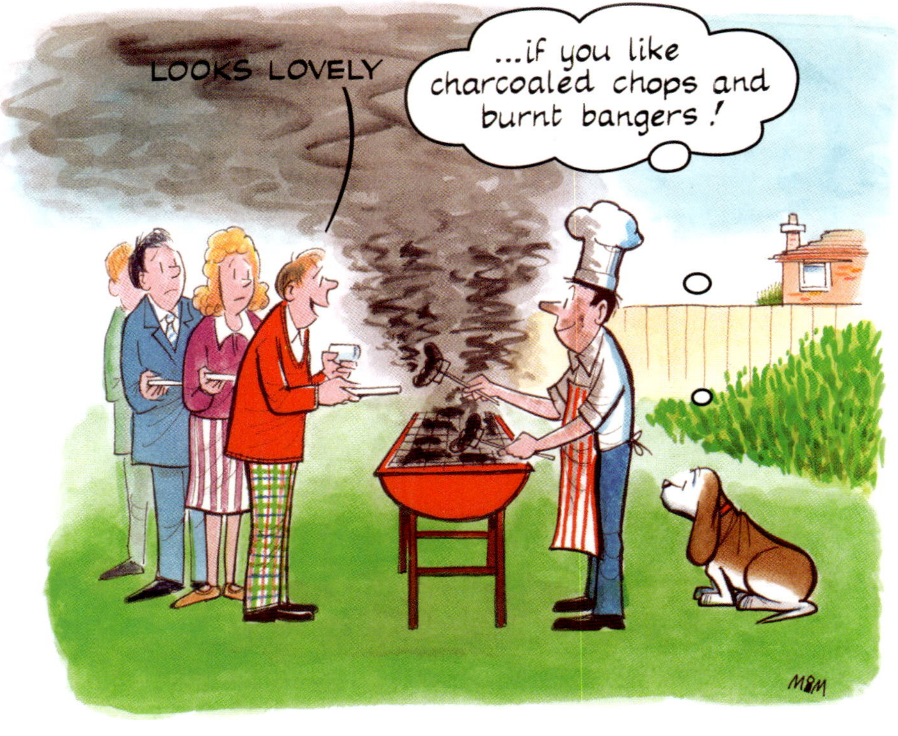
LOOKS LOVELY
...if you like charcoaled chops and burnt bangers!
M&M

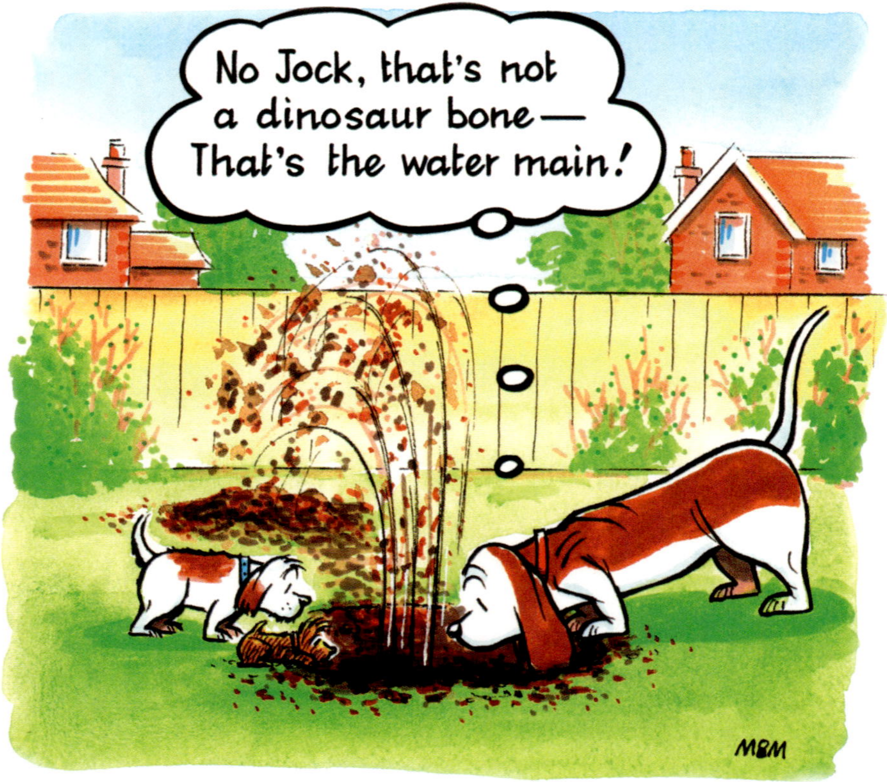
No Jock, that's not a dinosaur bone— That's the water main!
MBM

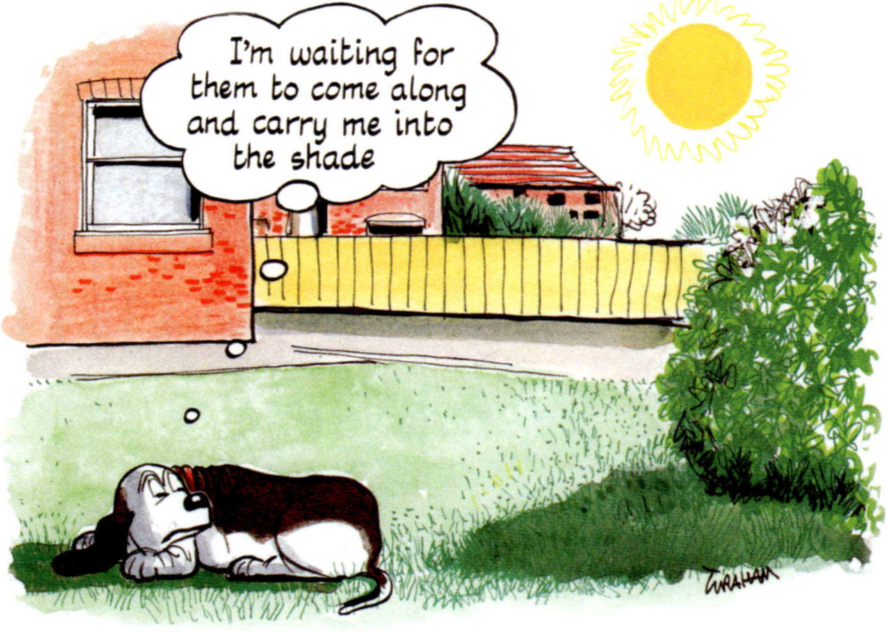
I'm waiting for them to come along and carry me into the shade
GRAHAM

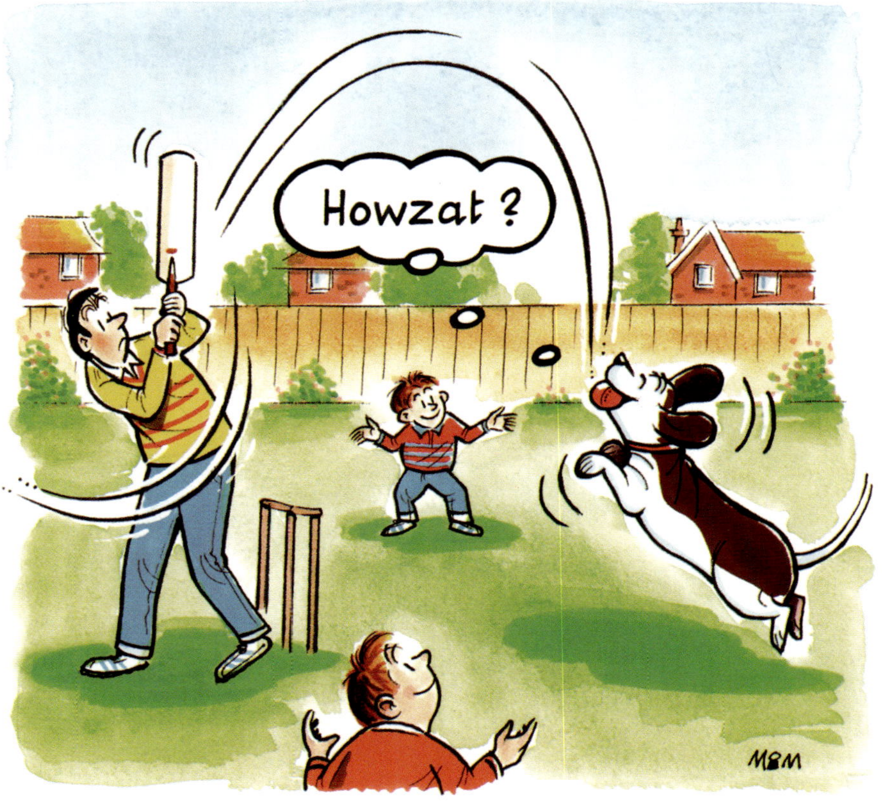
Howzat ?
M&M

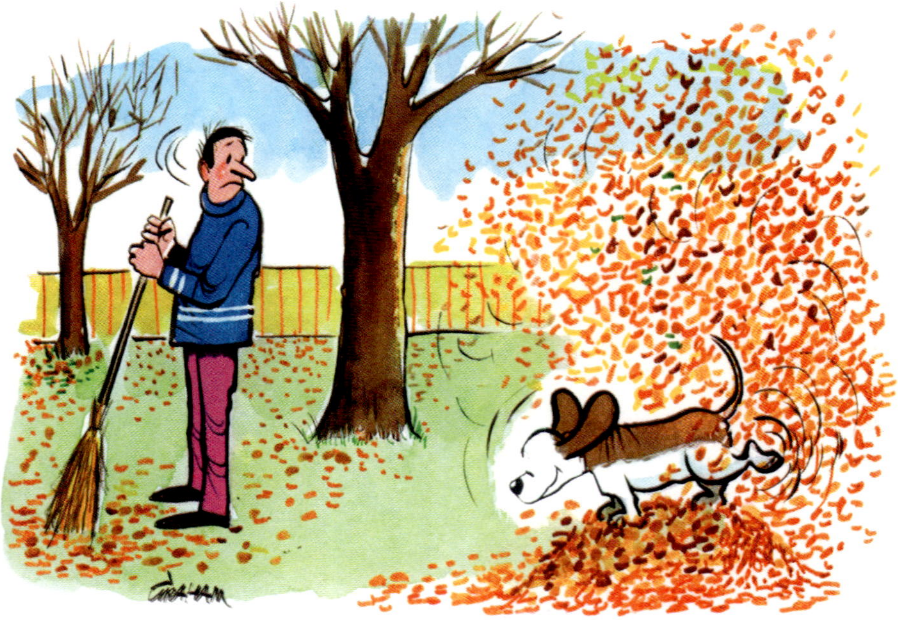

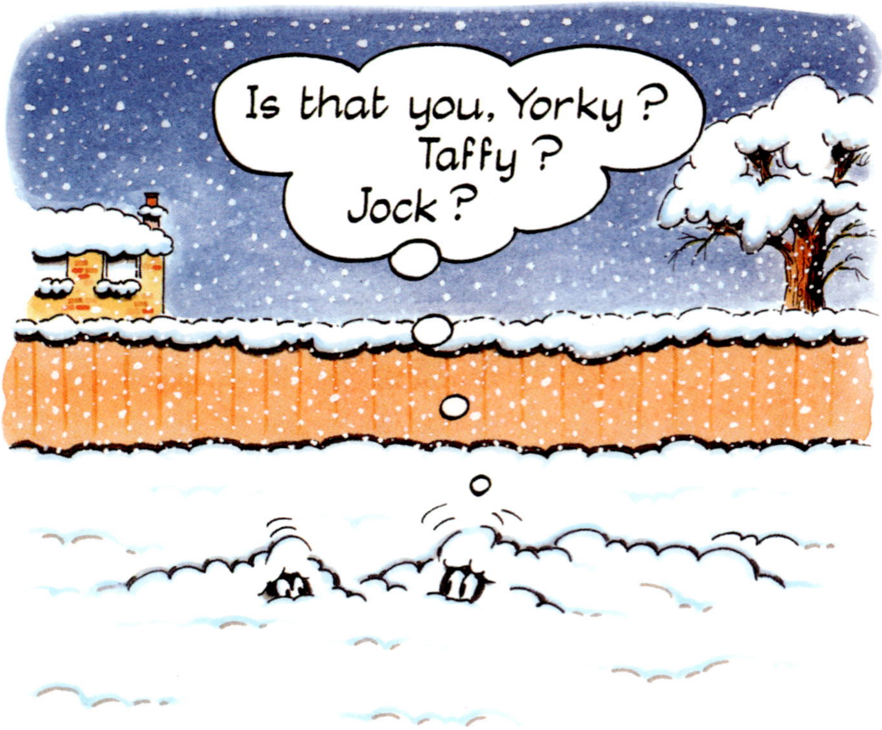
Is that you, Yorky?
Taffy?
Jock?

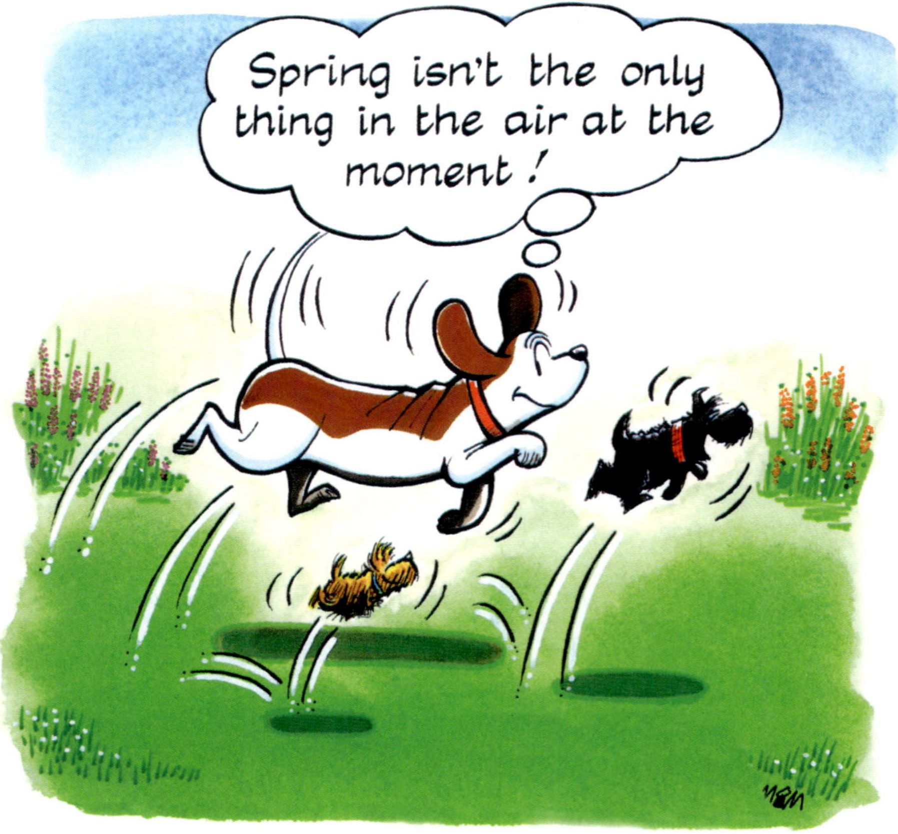
Spring isn't the only thing in the air at the moment!

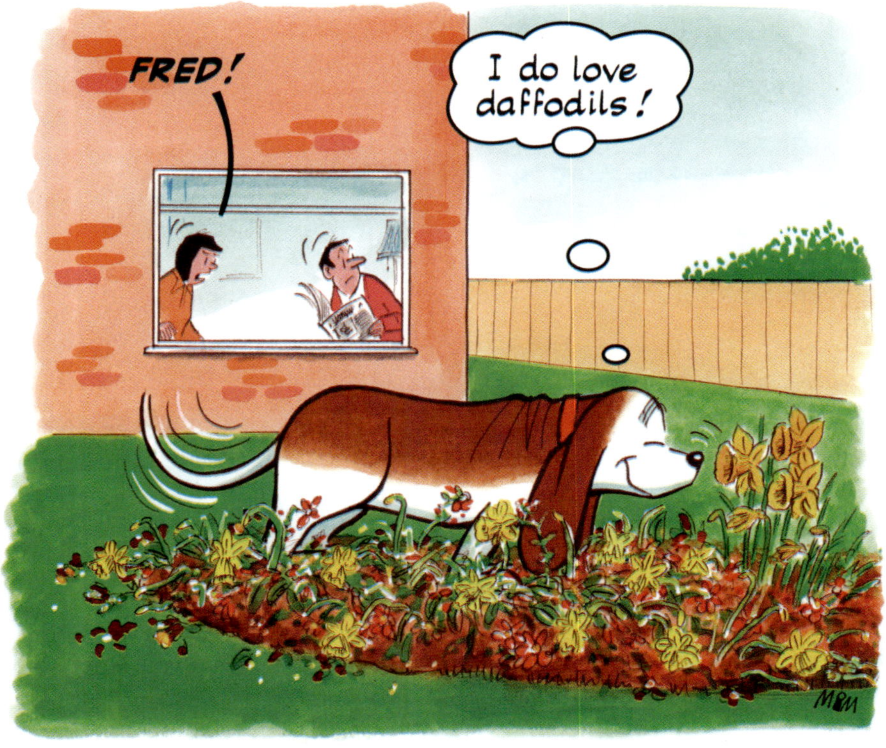
FRED!
I do love daffodils!
MCM

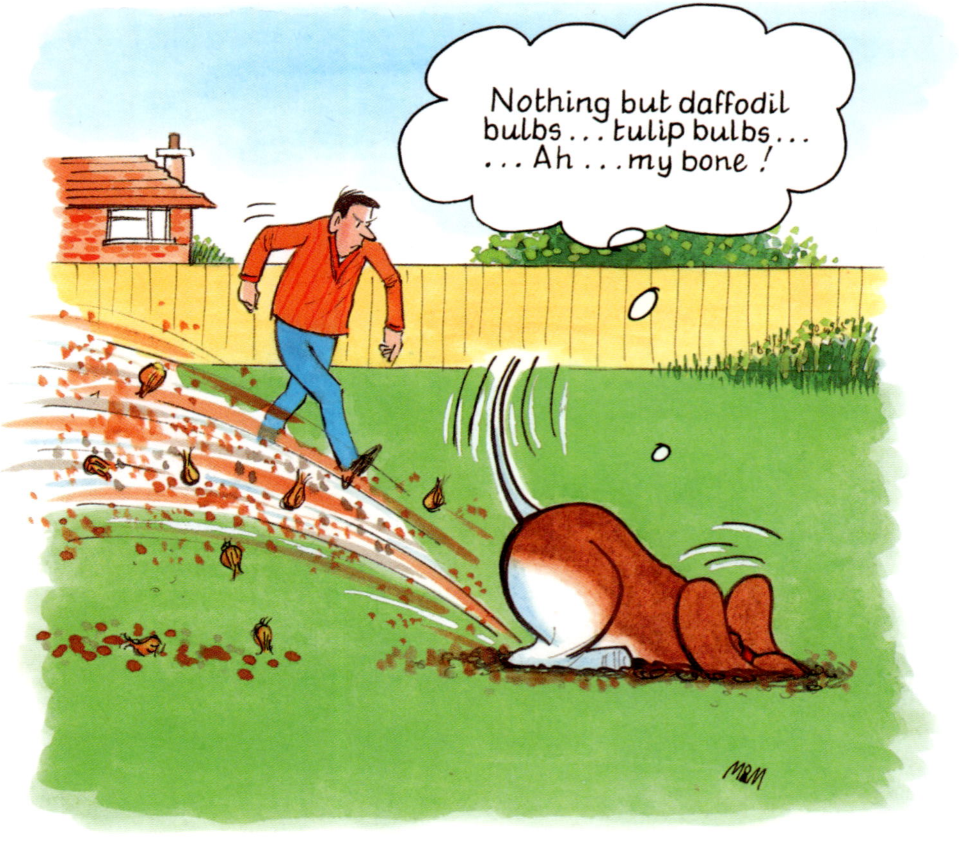
Nothing but daffodil bulbs . . . tulip bulbs . . . . . . Ah . . . my bone !
MGM

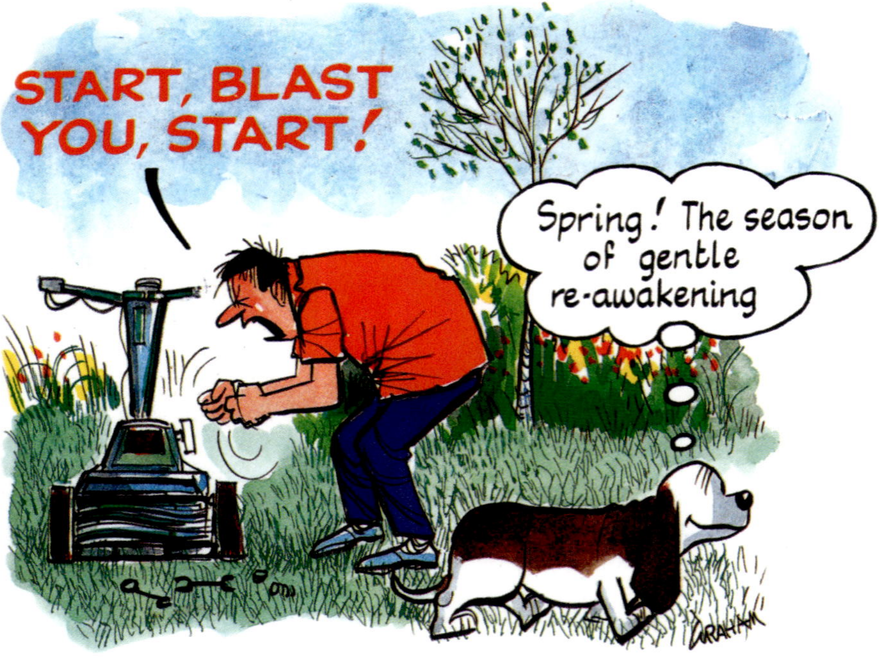
START, BLAST YOU, START!
Spring! The season of gentle re-awakening
GRAHAM

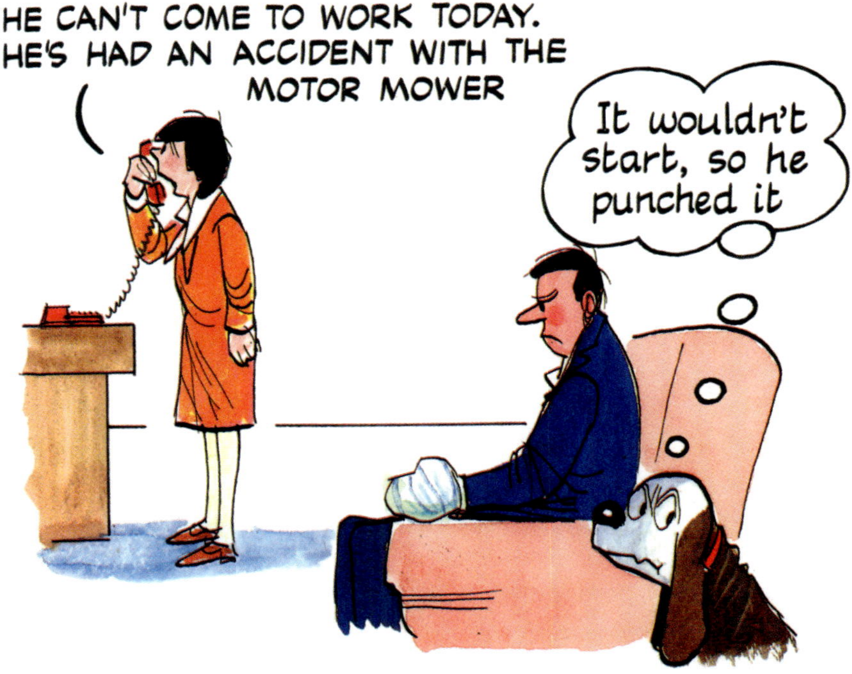
HE CAN'T COME TO WORK TODAY. HE'S HAD AN ACCIDENT WITH THE MOTOR MOWER
It wouldn't start, so he punched it

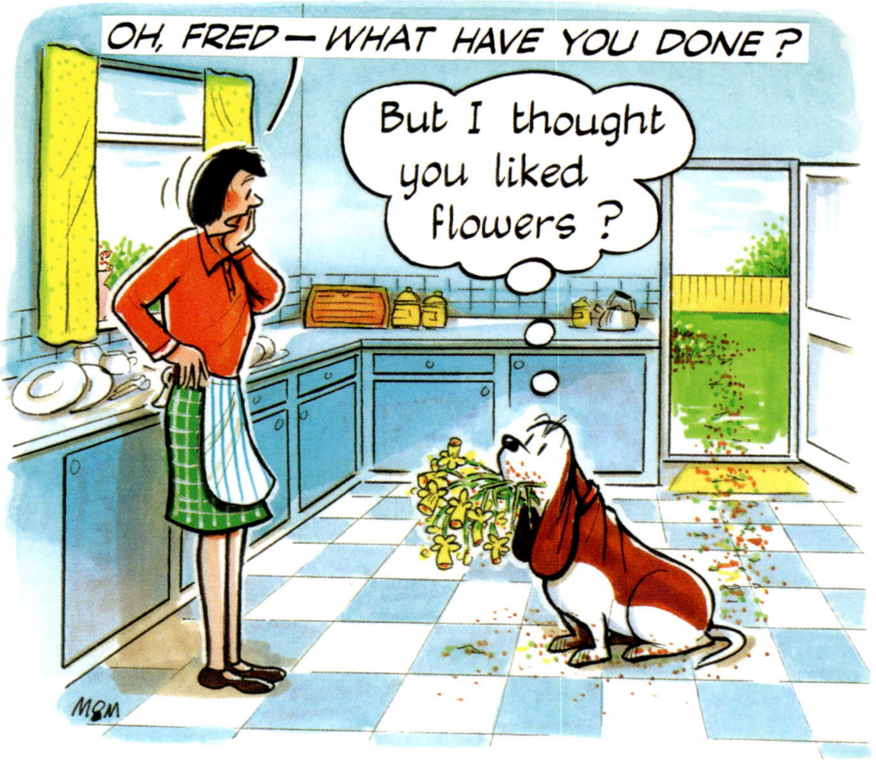
OH, FRED — WHAT HAVE YOU DONE?
But I thought you liked flowers?
MGM

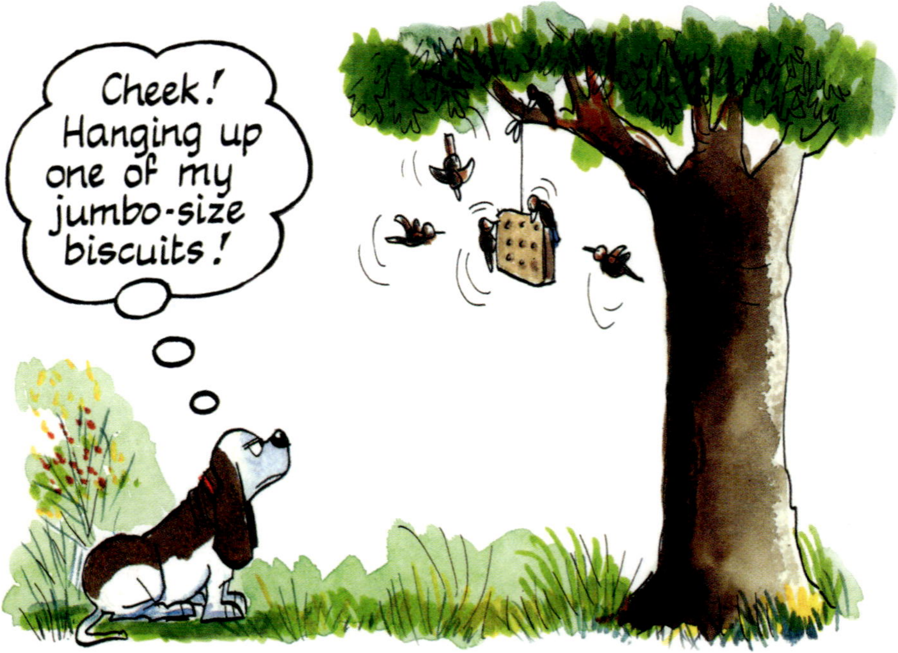
Cheek! Hanging up one of my jumbo-size biscuits!

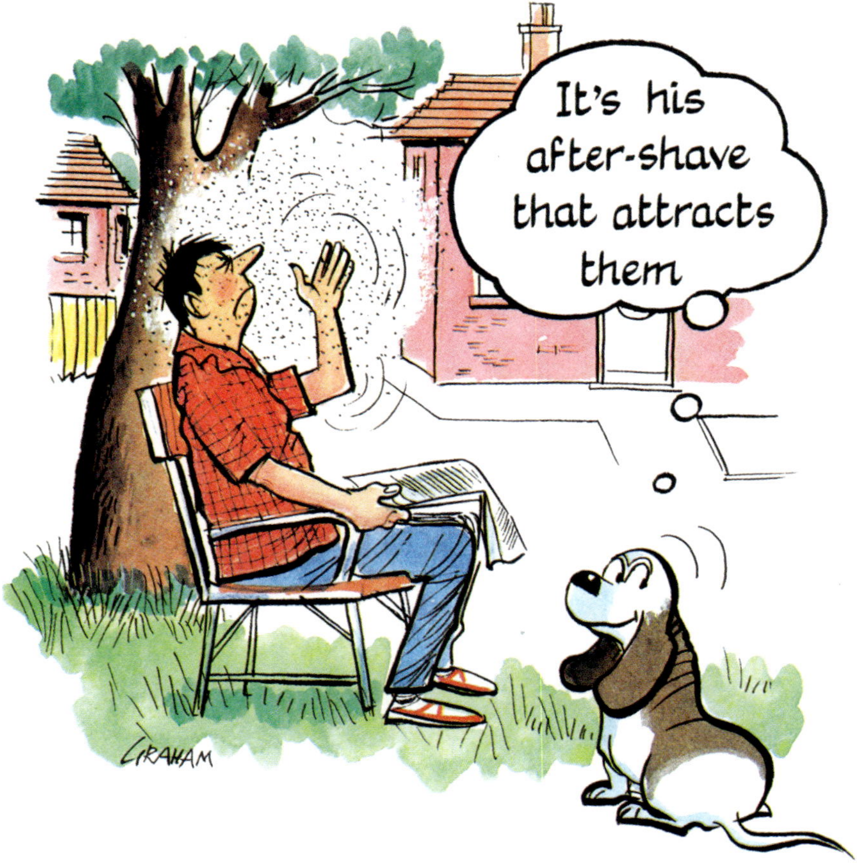
It's his after-shave that attracts them
GRAHAM

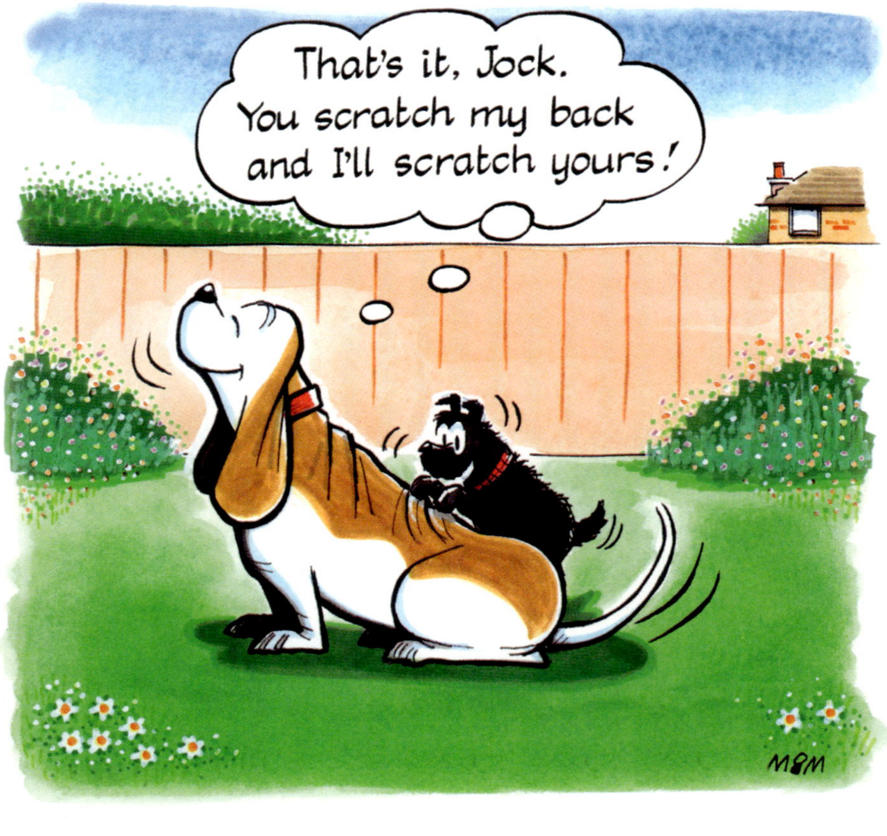
That's it, Jock.
You scratch my back
and I'll scratch yours!
M&M

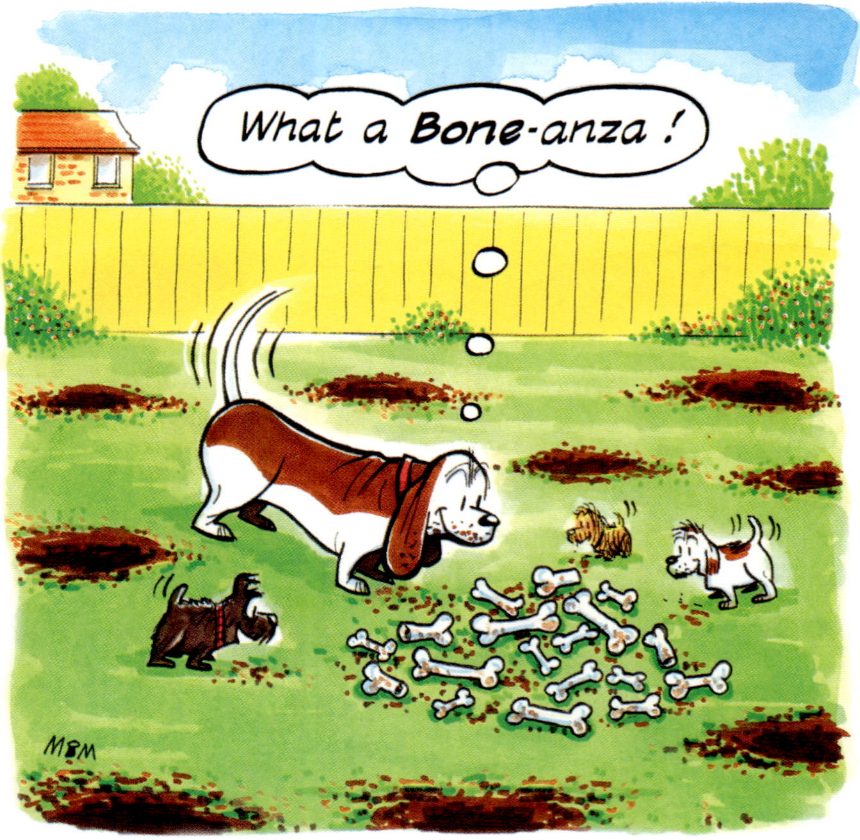
What a Bone-anza !
MBM

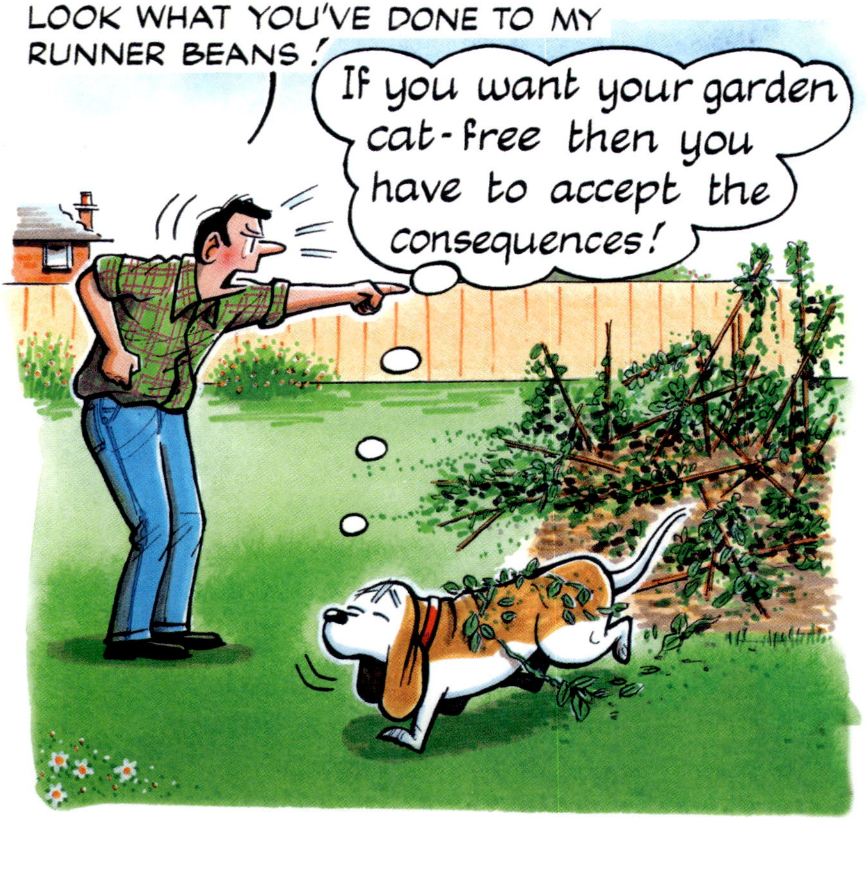

LOOK WHAT YOU'VE DONE TO MY RUNNER BEANS!
If you want your garden cat-free then you have to accept the consequences!

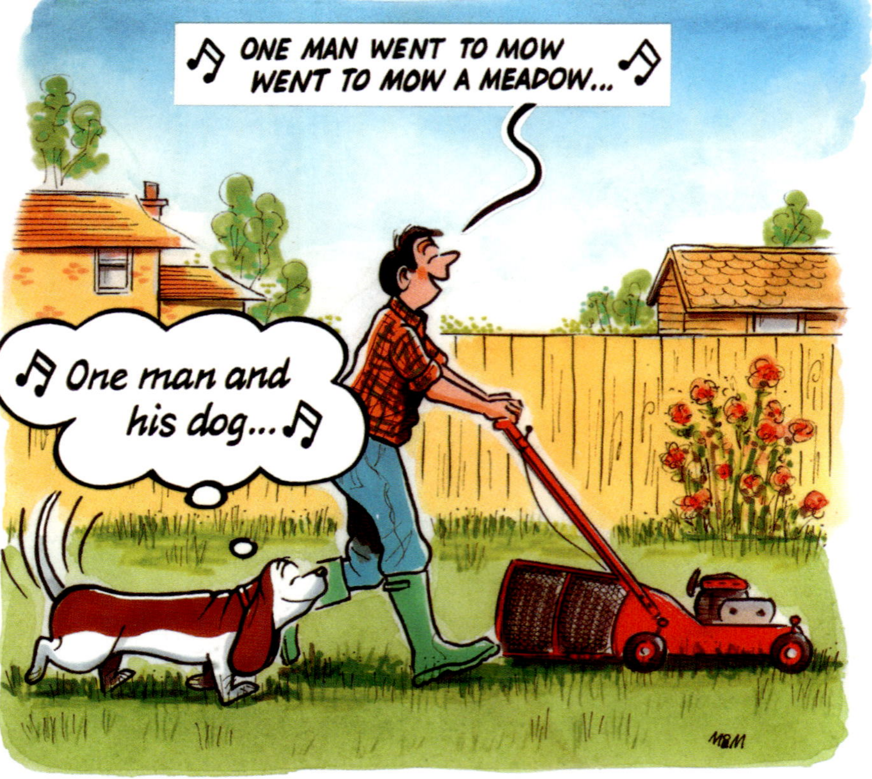
ONE MAN WENT TO MOW
WENT TO MOW A MEADOW...
One man and his dog...
M&M

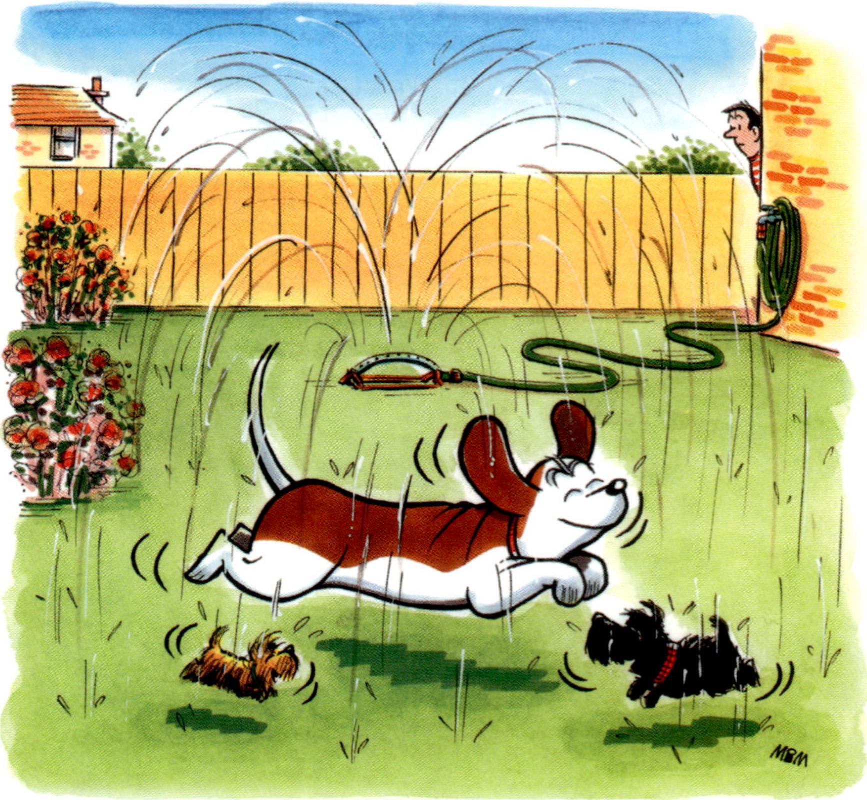

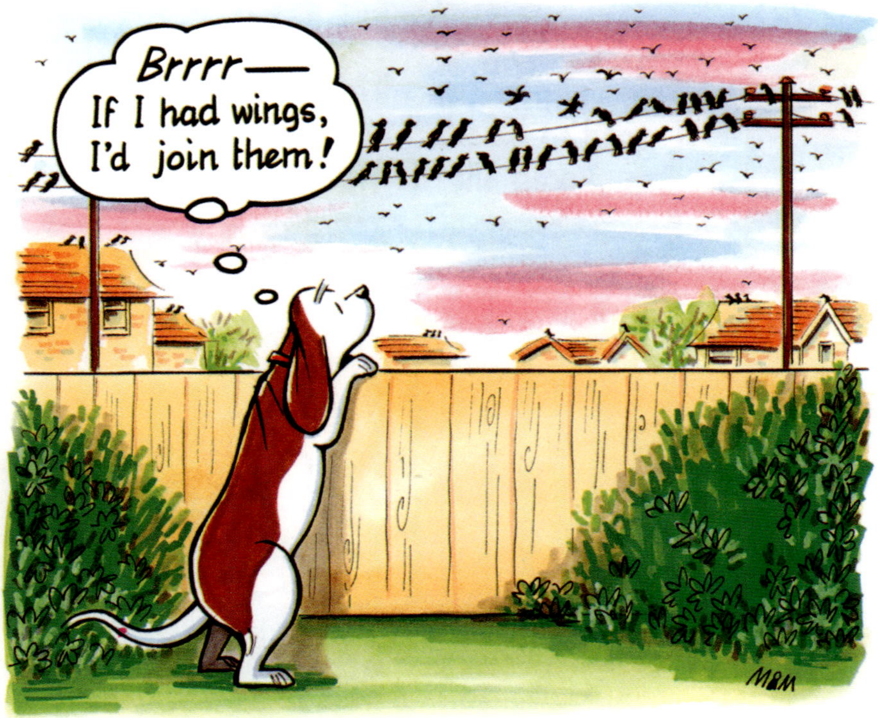
Brrrr—
If I had wings,
I'd join them!
M&M

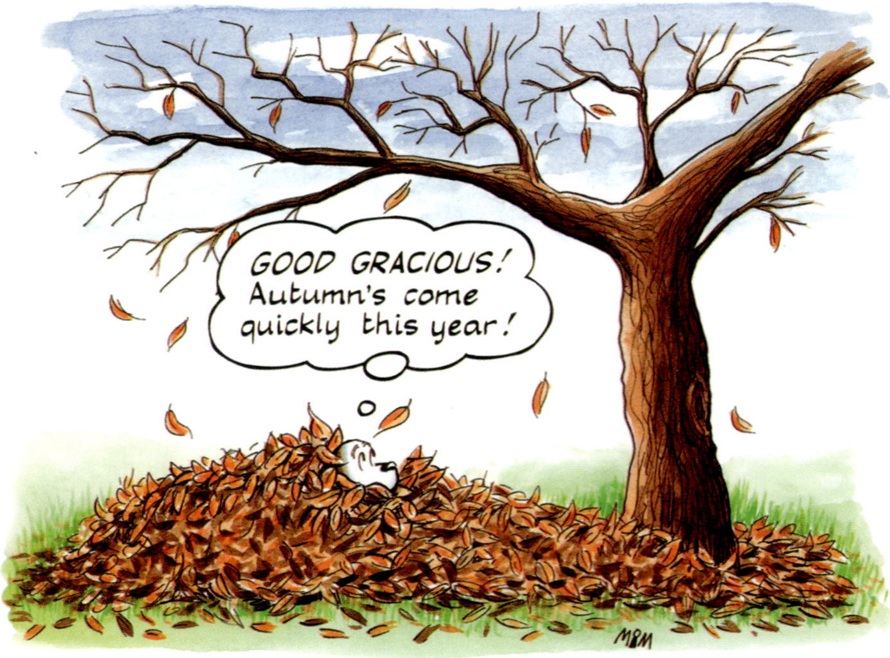
GOOD GRACIOUS! Autumn's come quickly this year!
M&M

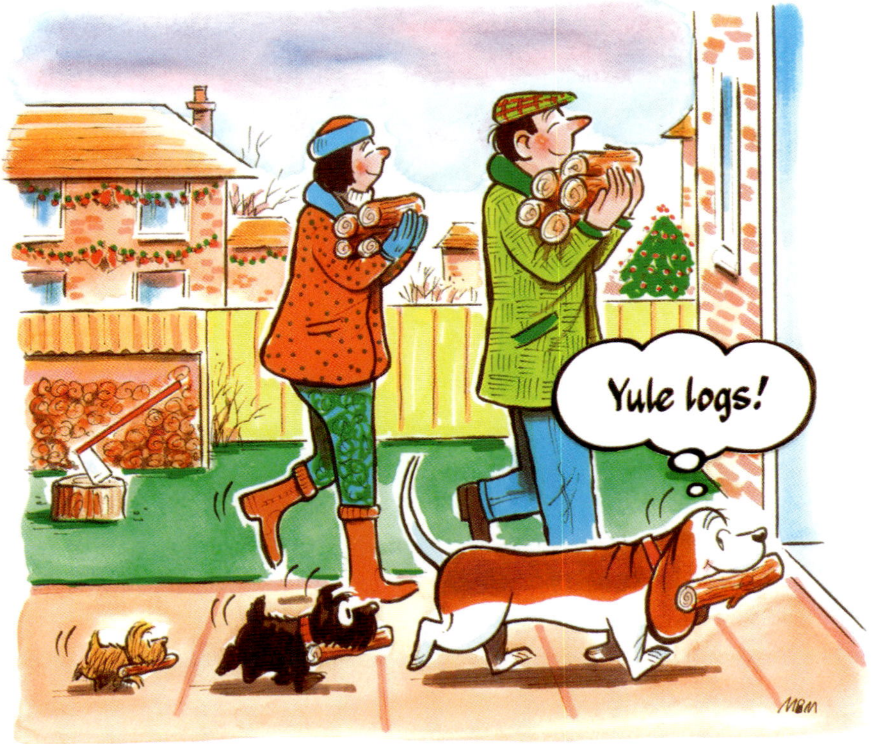
Yule logs!
MBM

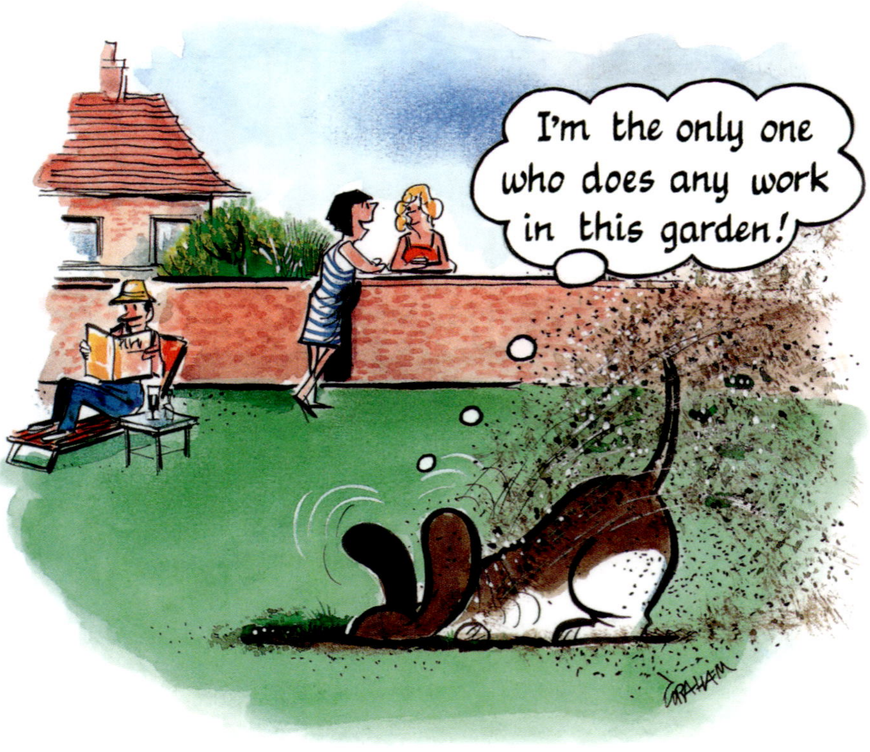
I'm the only one who does any work in this garden!
GRAHAM

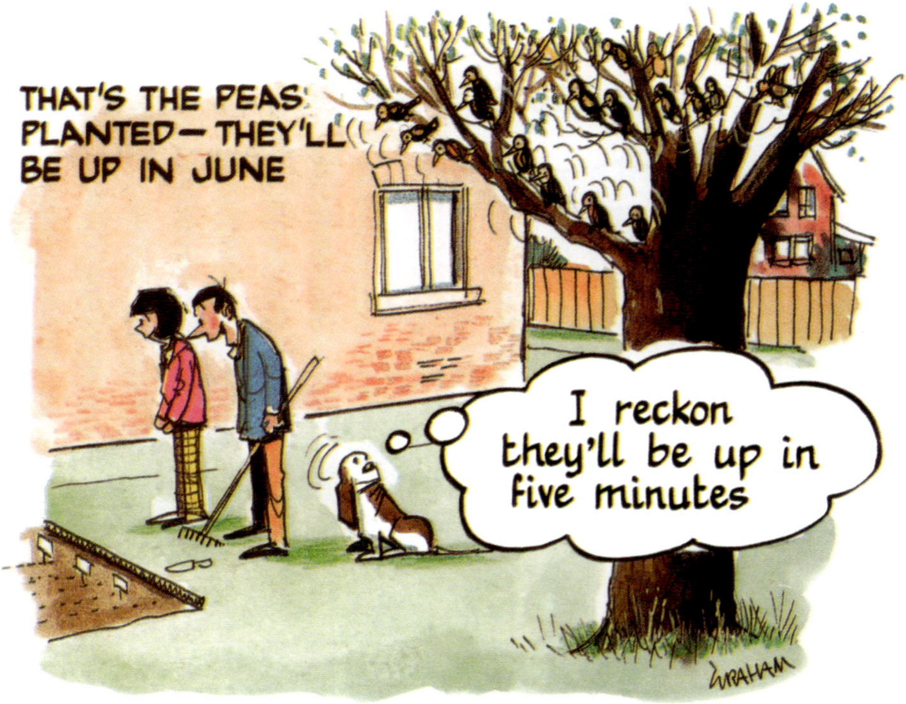
THAT'S THE PEAS PLANTED— THEY'LL BE UP IN JUNE
I reckon they'll be up in five minutes
GRAHAM

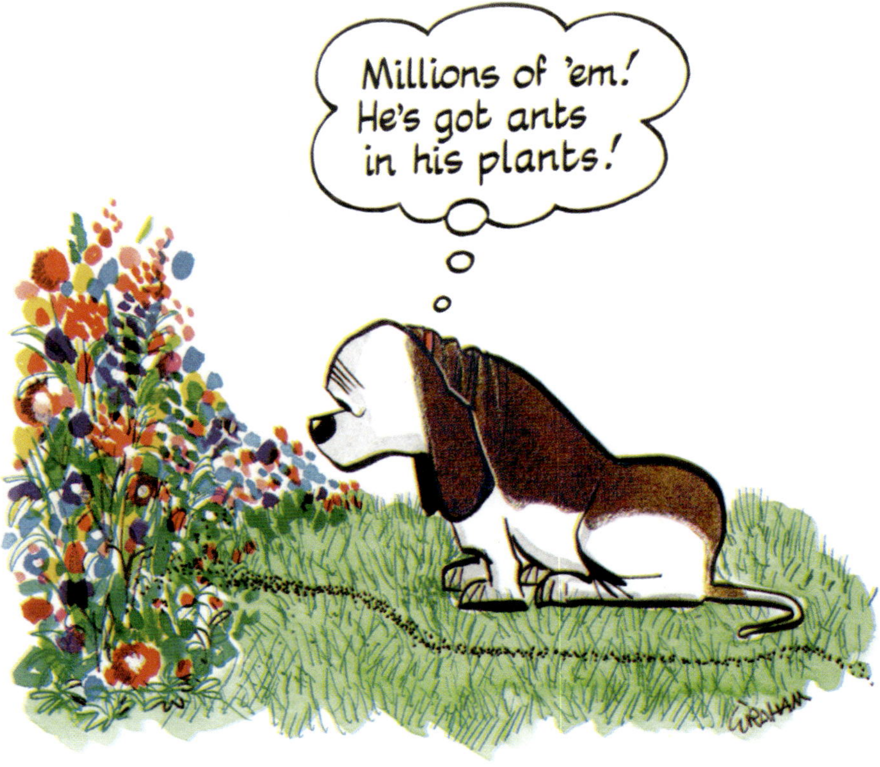
Millions of 'em! He's got ants in his plants!
GRAHAM

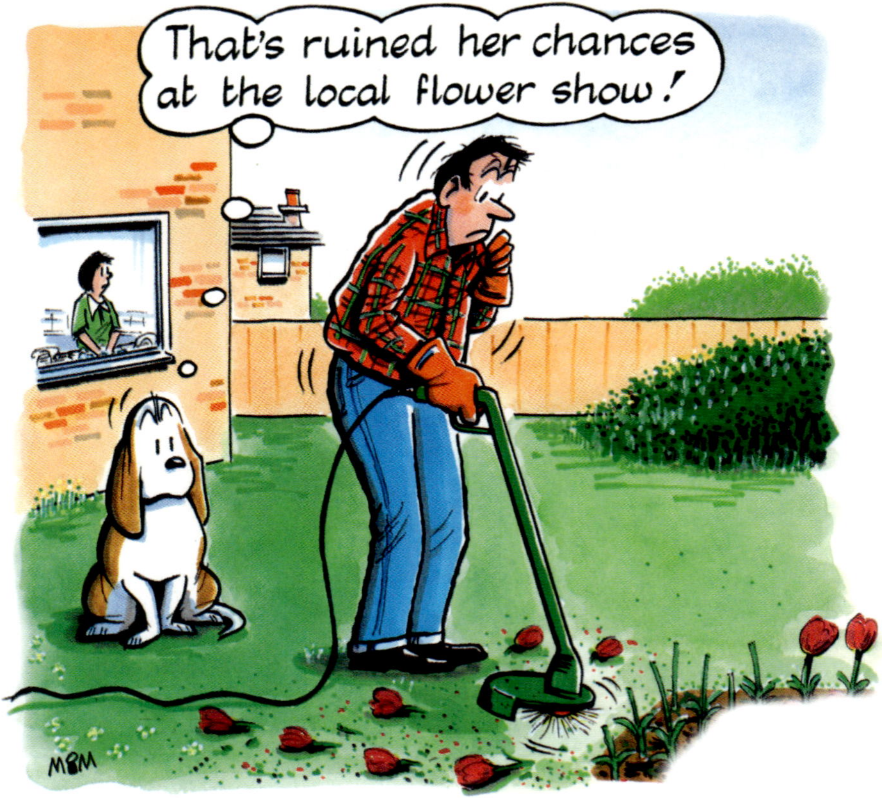
That's ruined her chances at the local flower show!
MBM

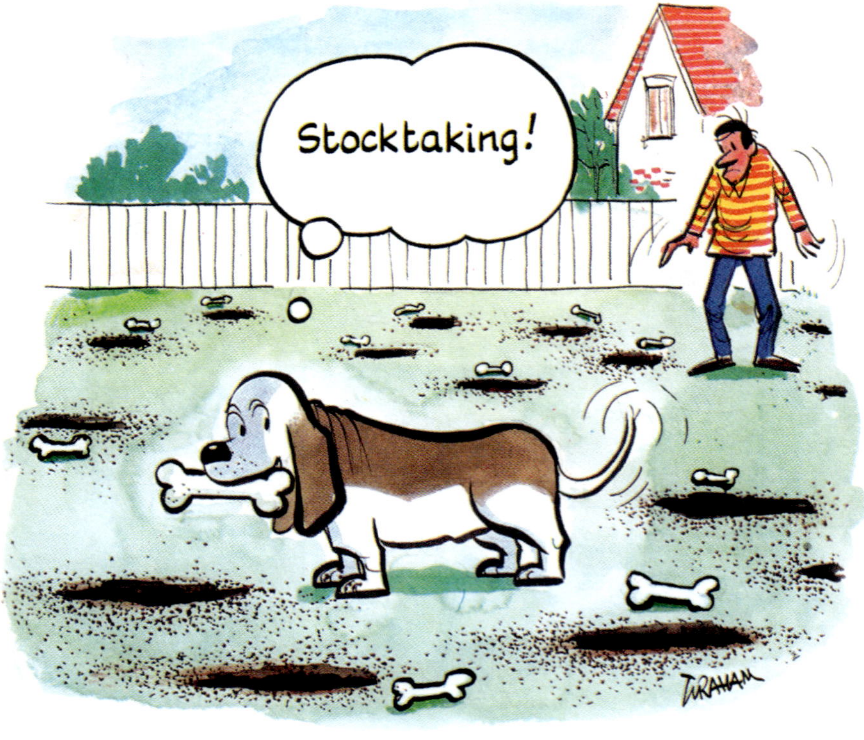
Stocktaking!
GRAHAM

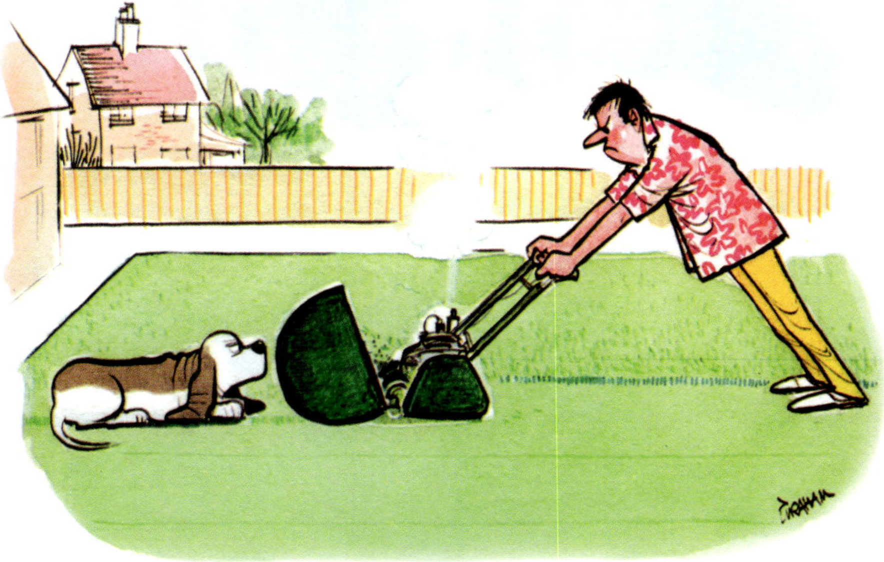
GRAHAM

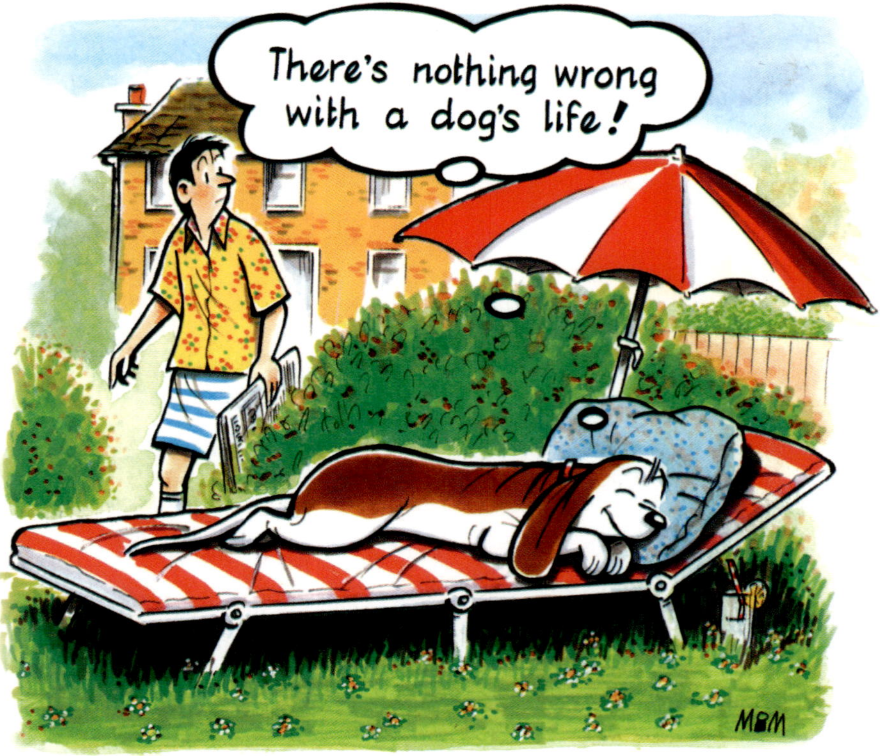
There's nothing wrong with a dog's life!
MBM

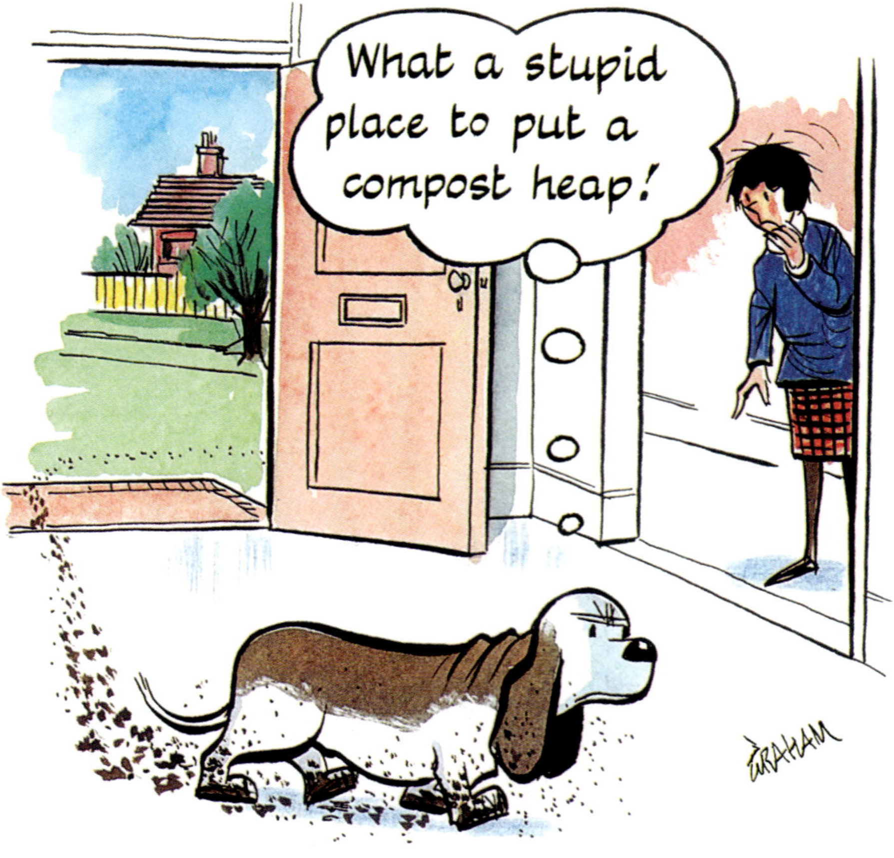
What a stupid place to put a compost heap!
GRAHAM

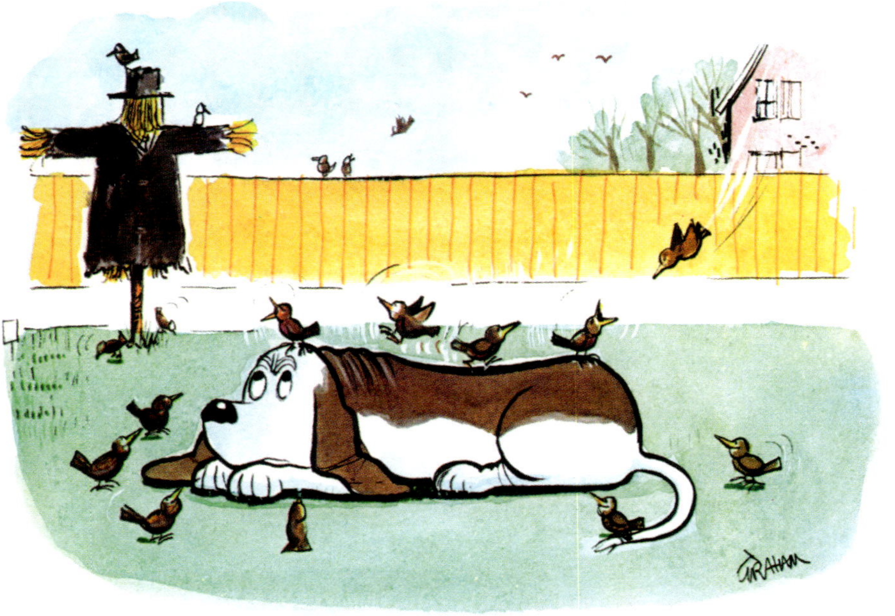
GRAHAM

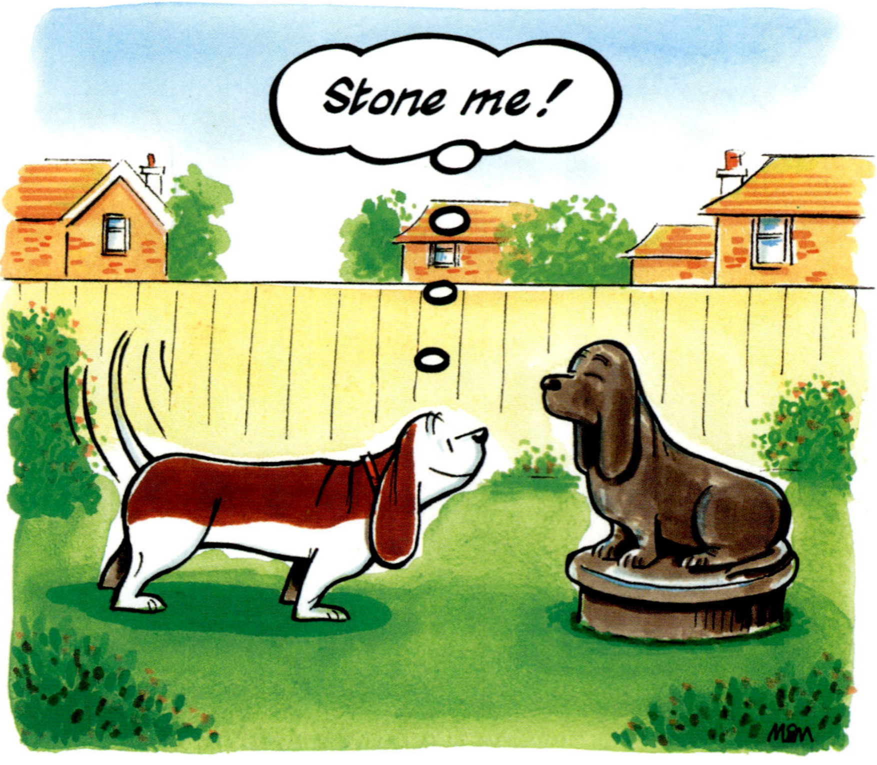
Stone me!
MCM

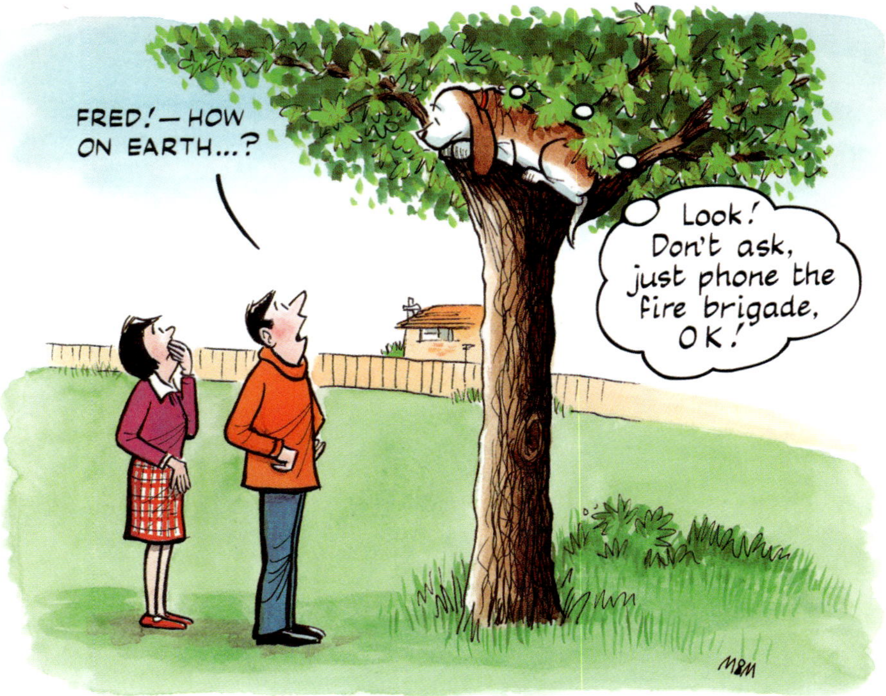
FRED! — HOW ON EARTH...?
Look! Don't ask, just phone the fire brigade, OK!
MBM

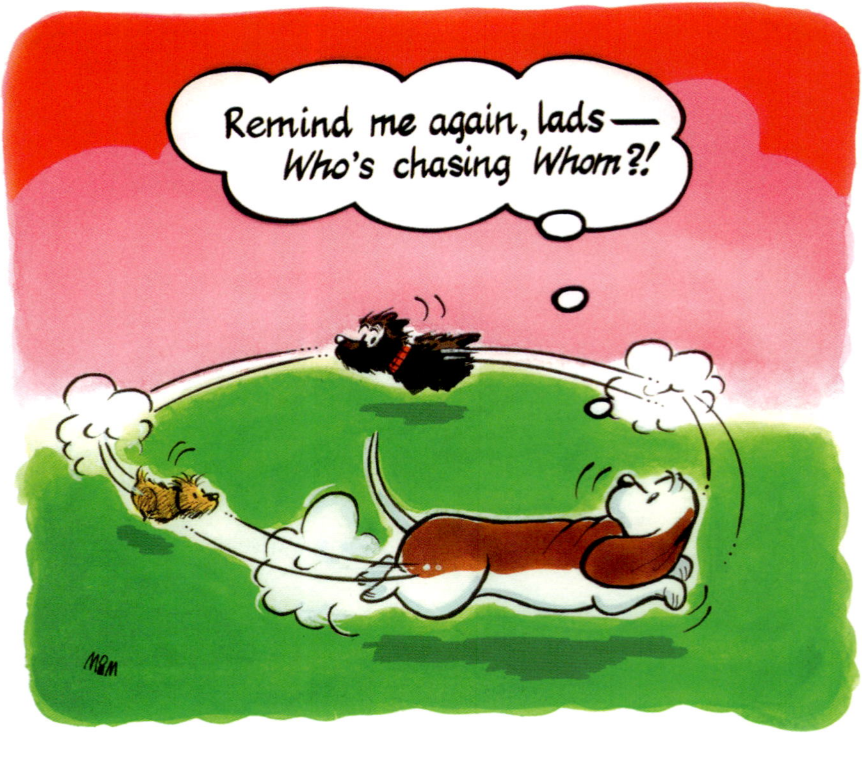
Remind me again, lads—
Who's chasing Whom?!
MGM

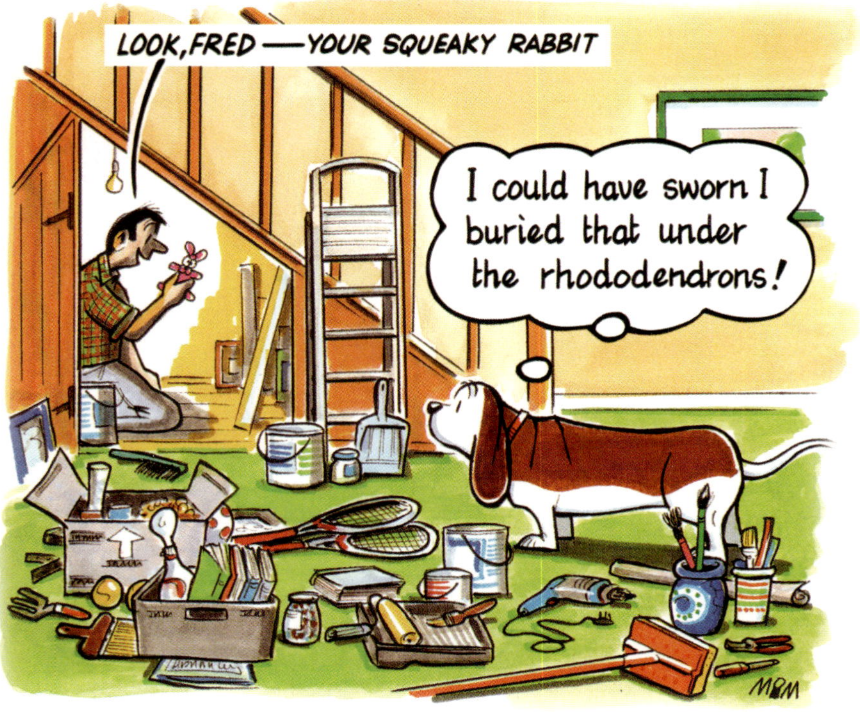
LOOK, FRED — YOUR SQUEAKY RABBIT
I could have sworn I buried that under the rhododendrons!
M&M

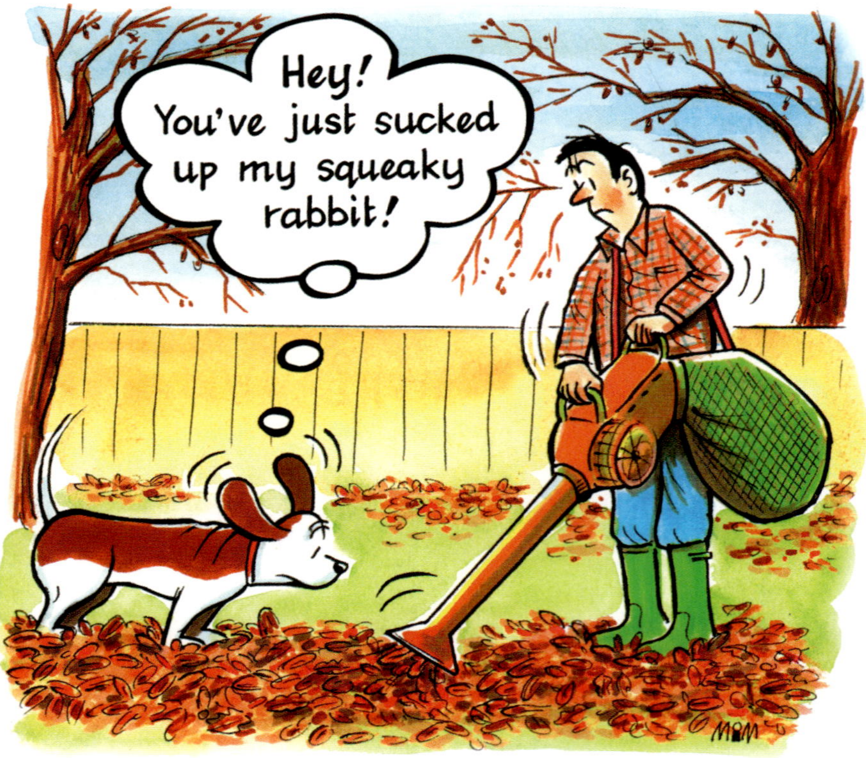
Hey! You've just sucked up my squeaky rabbit!
MPM

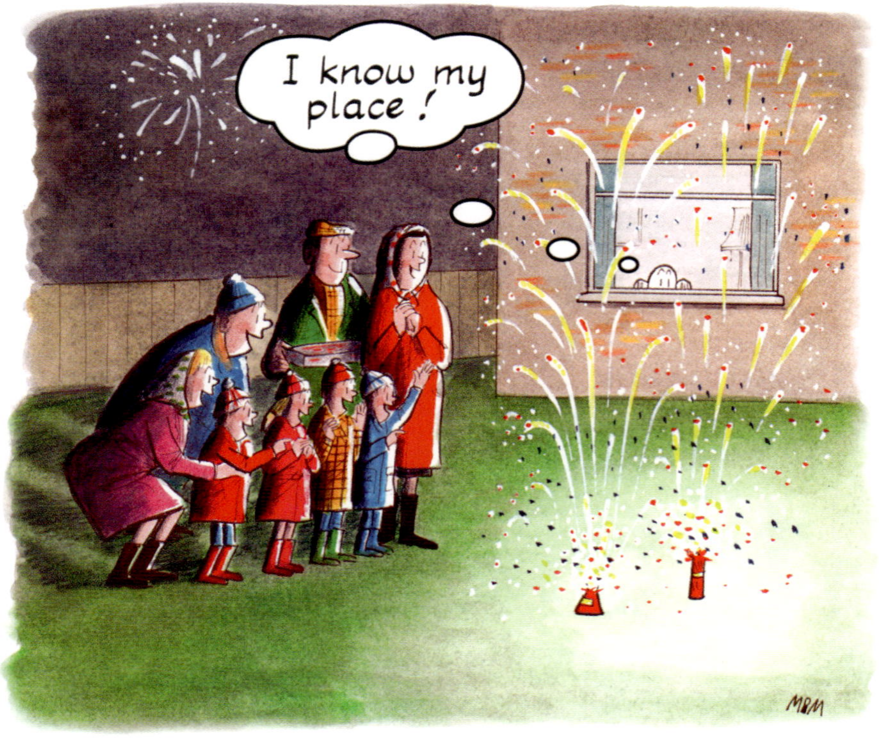
I know my place!
MBM

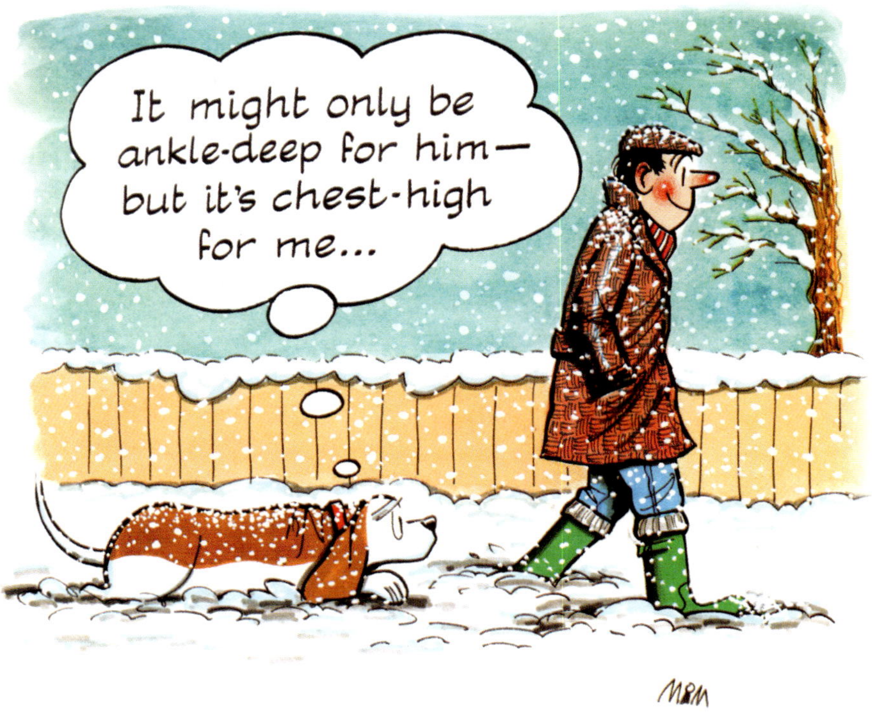
It might only be ankle-deep for him—but it's chest-high for me...
MRM

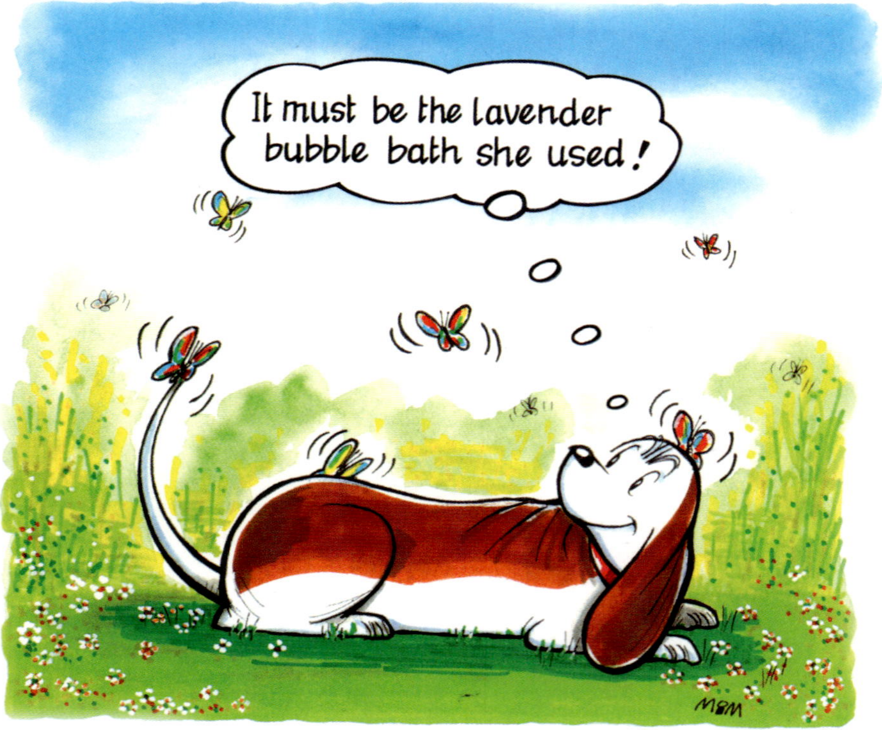
It must be the lavender bubble bath she used!
M&M

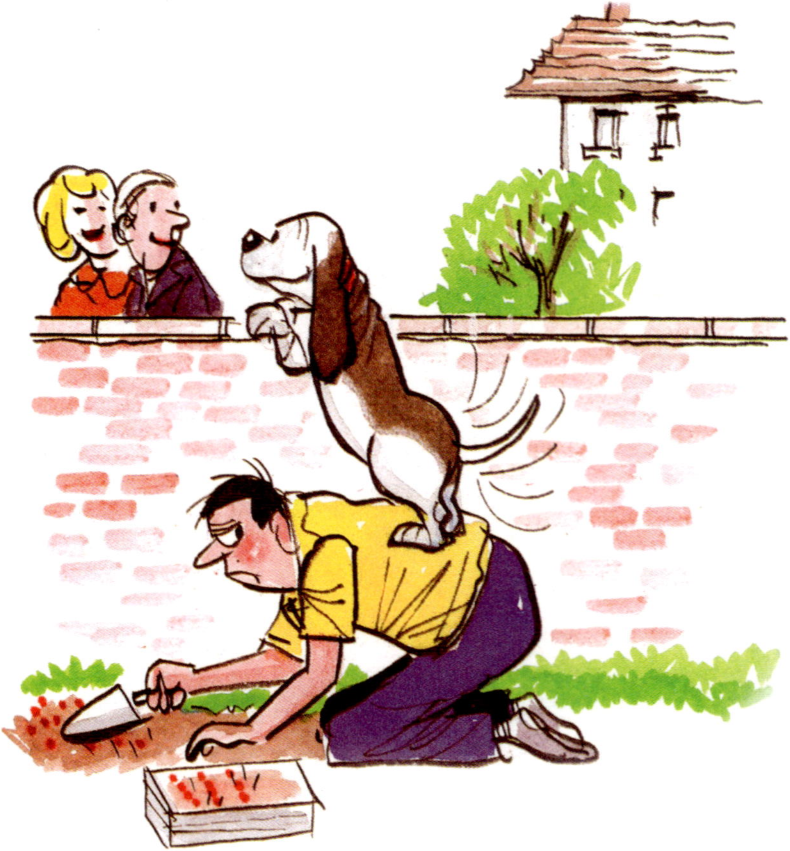

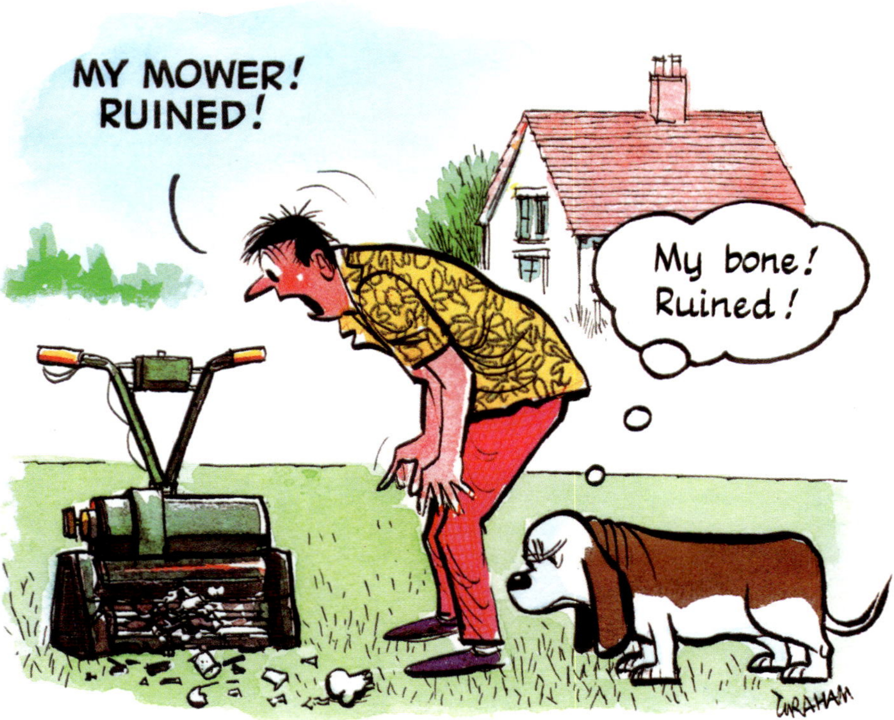
MY MOWER! RUINED!
My bone! Ruined!
GRAHAM

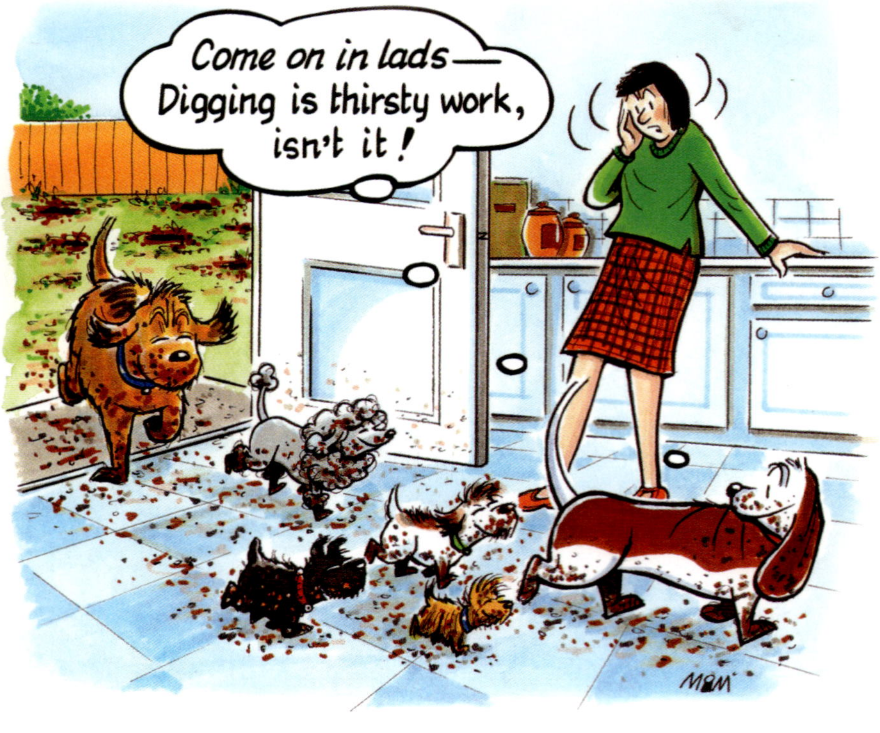
Come on in lads—
Digging is thirsty work,
isn't it!
MGM

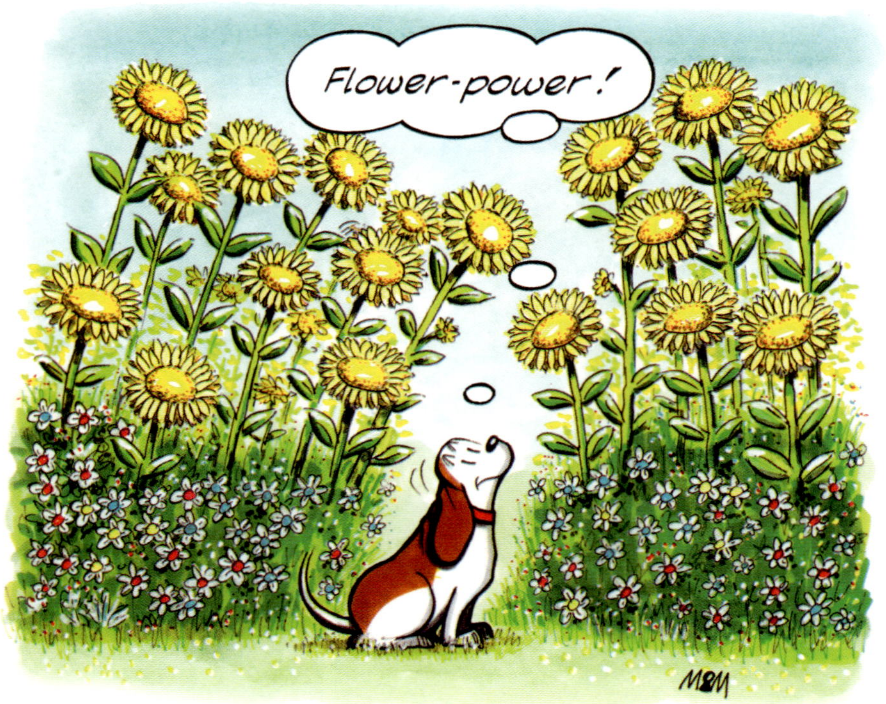
Flower-power!
M&M

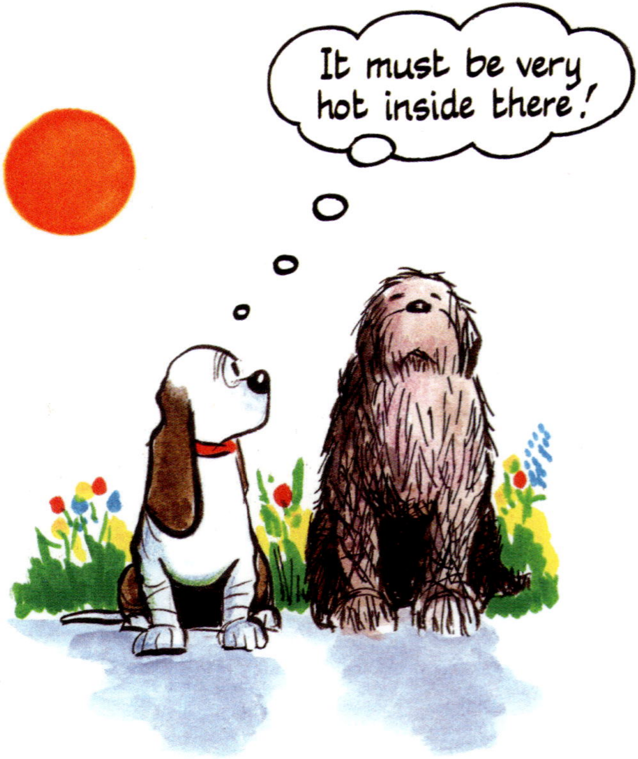
It must be very hot inside there!

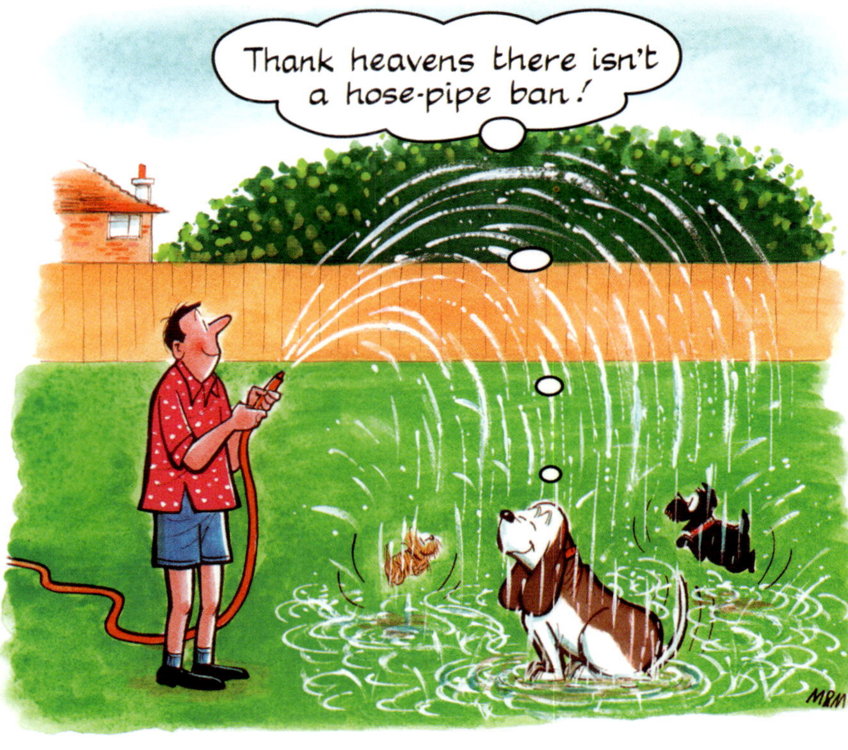
Thank heavens there isn't a hose-pipe ban!
MPM

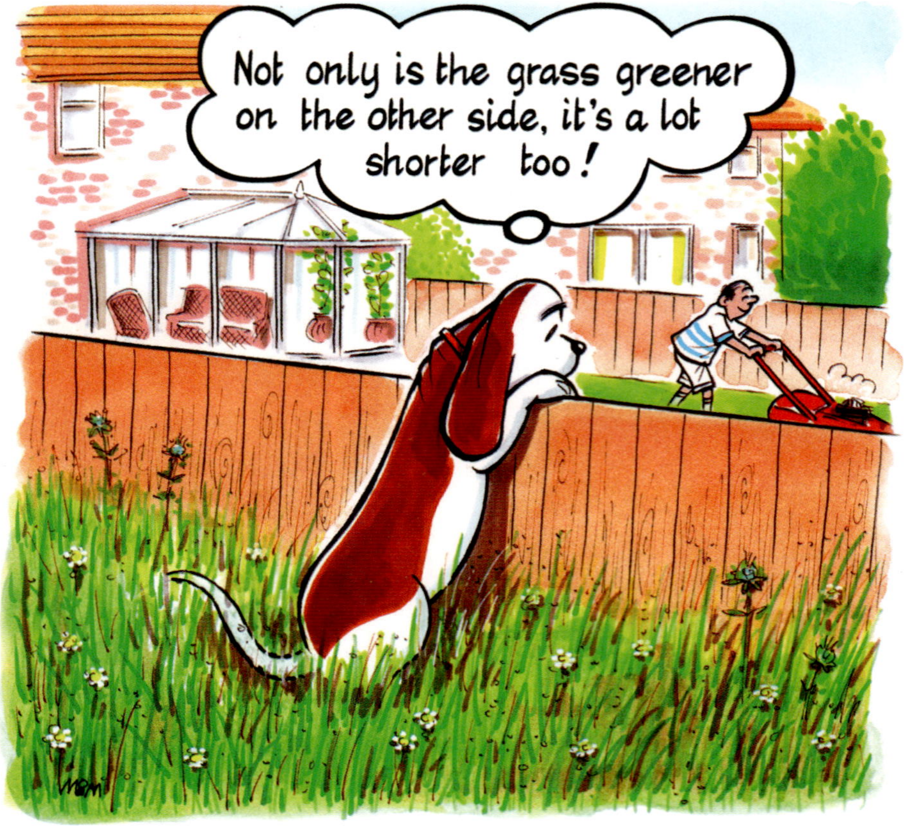
Not only is the grass greener on the other side, it's a lot shorter too!

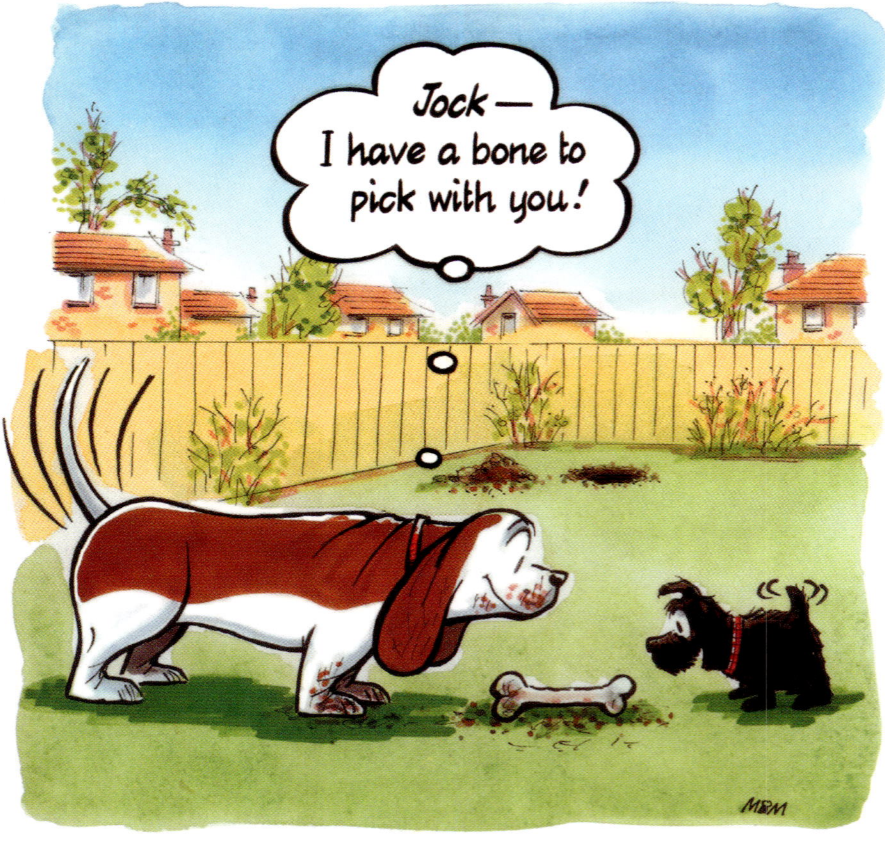
Jock —
I have a bone to pick with you!
M&M

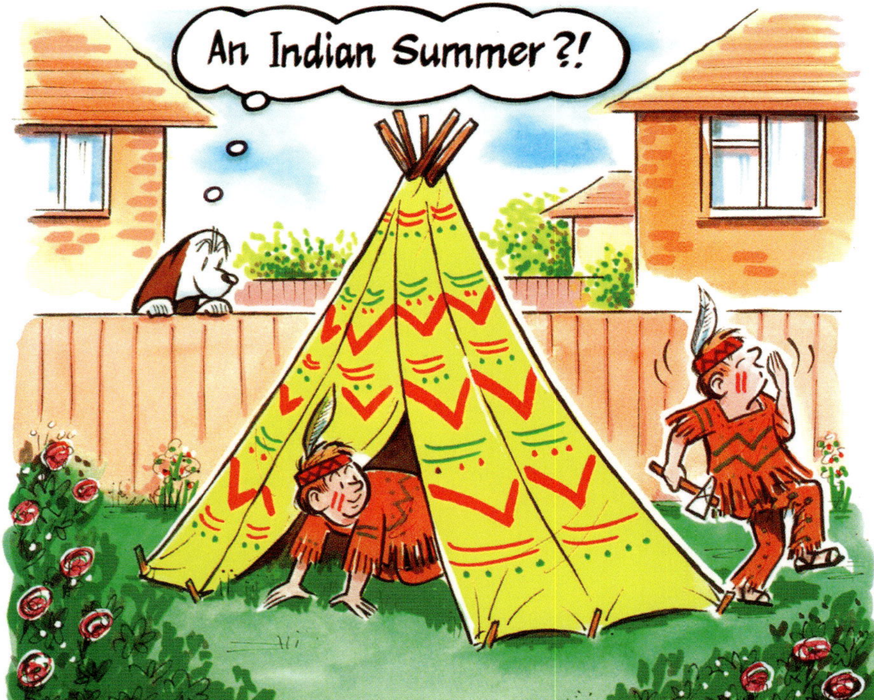
An Indian Summer?!

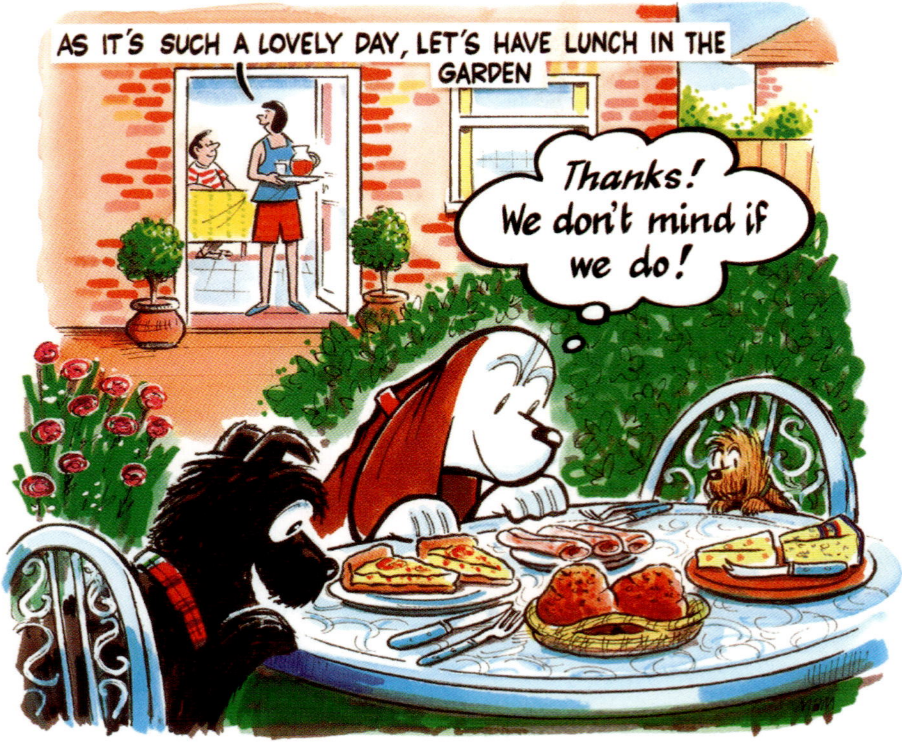
AS IT'S SUCH A LOVELY DAY, LET'S HAVE LUNCH IN THE GARDEN
Thanks! We don't mind if we do!

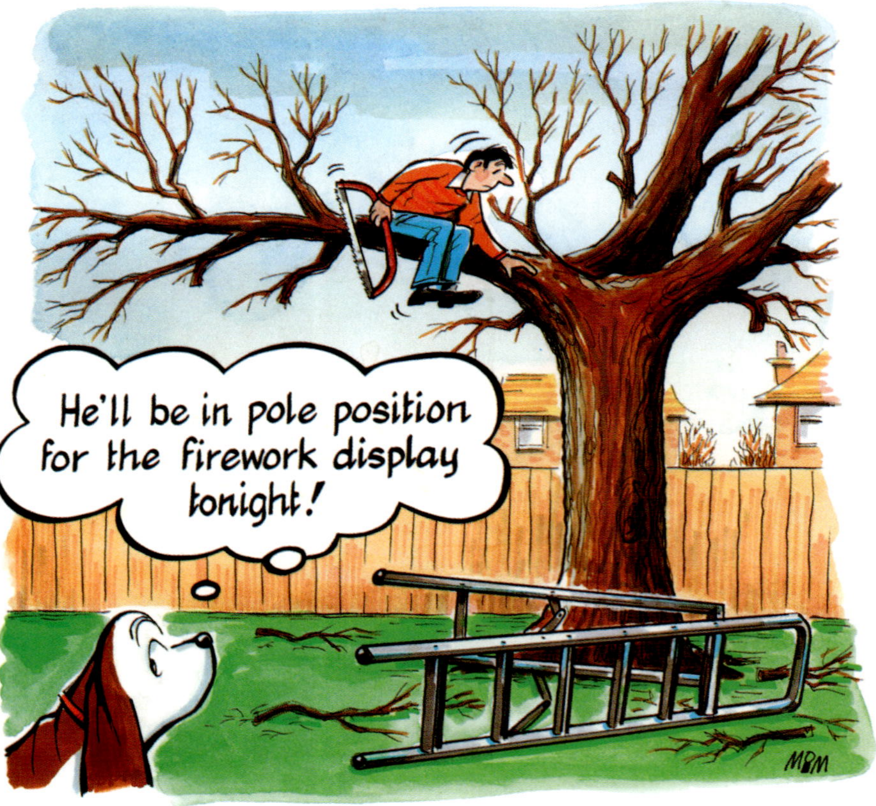
He'll be in pole position for the firework display tonight!
MBM

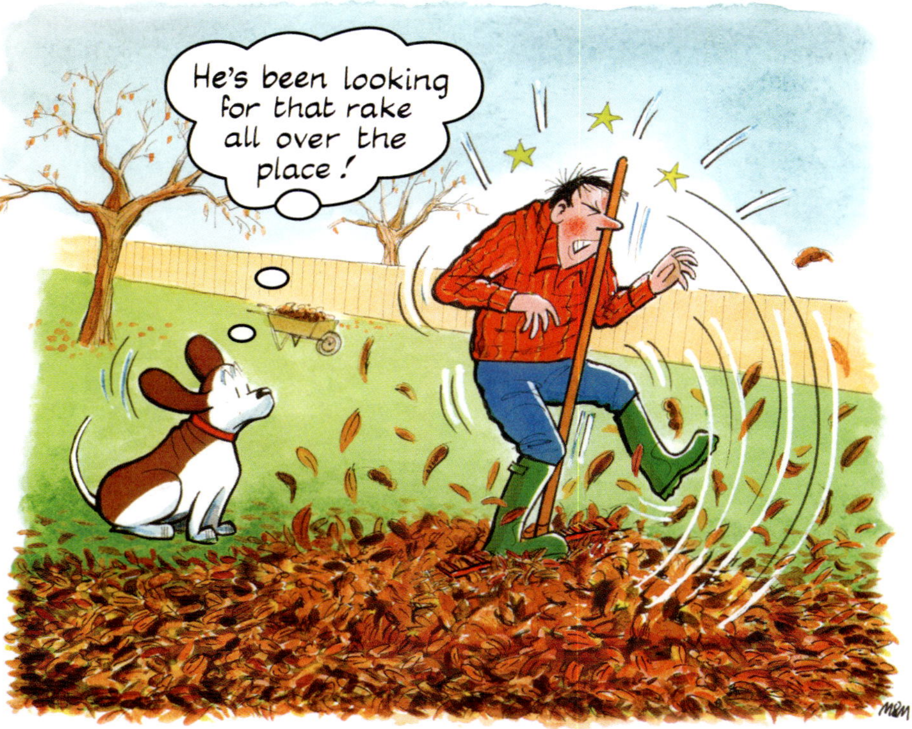
He's been looking for that rake all over the place!
M&M

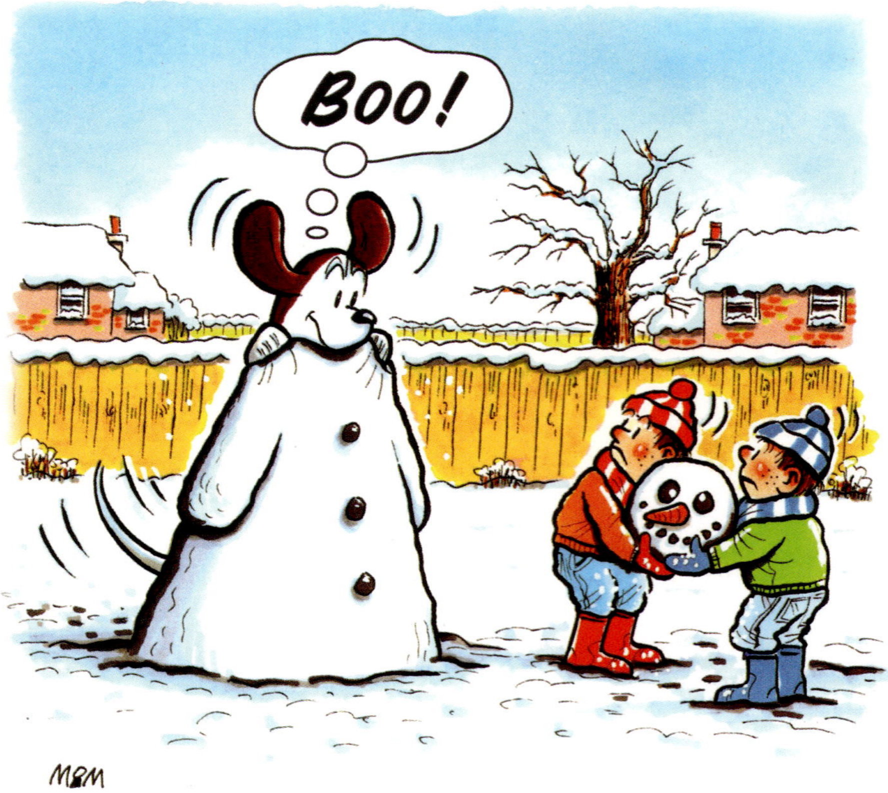BOO!
M&M

Look out for more Fred Basset gift books coming soon...

Have you enjoyed this book? If so, why not
write a review on your favourite website?

Thanks very much for buying
this Summersdale book.

www.summersdale.com

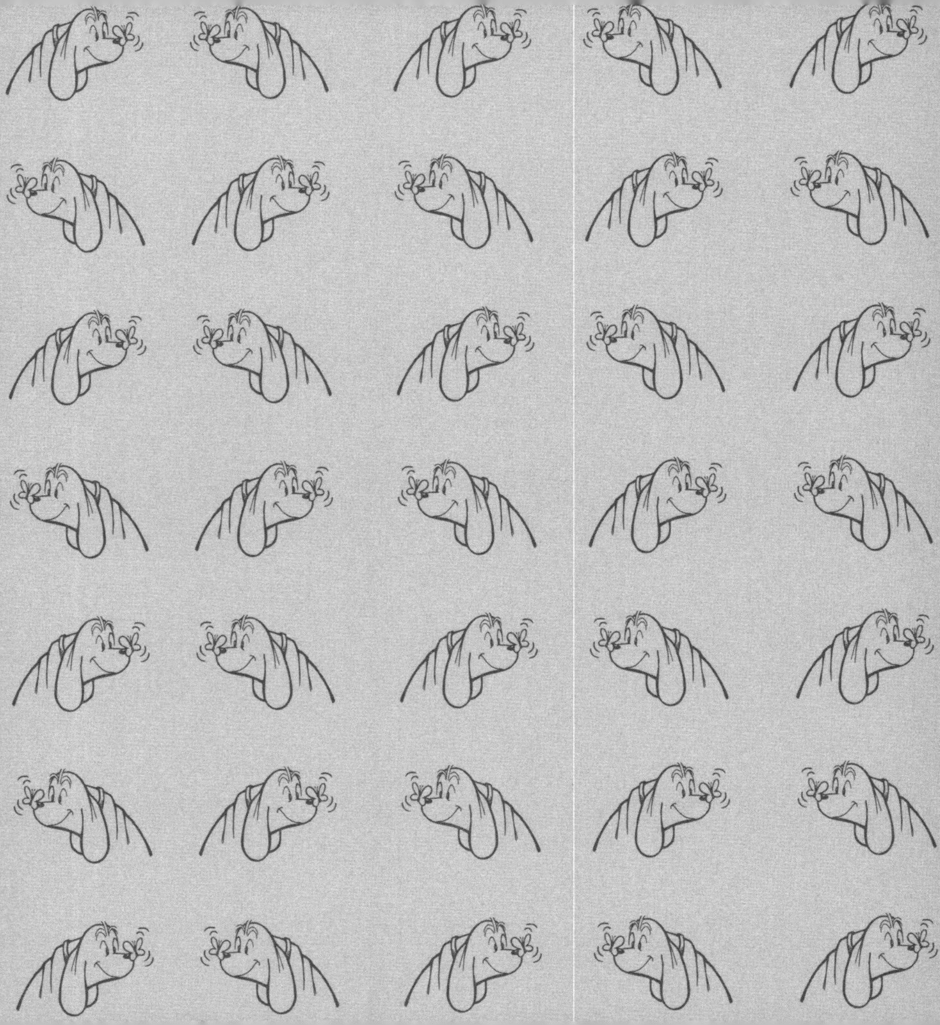

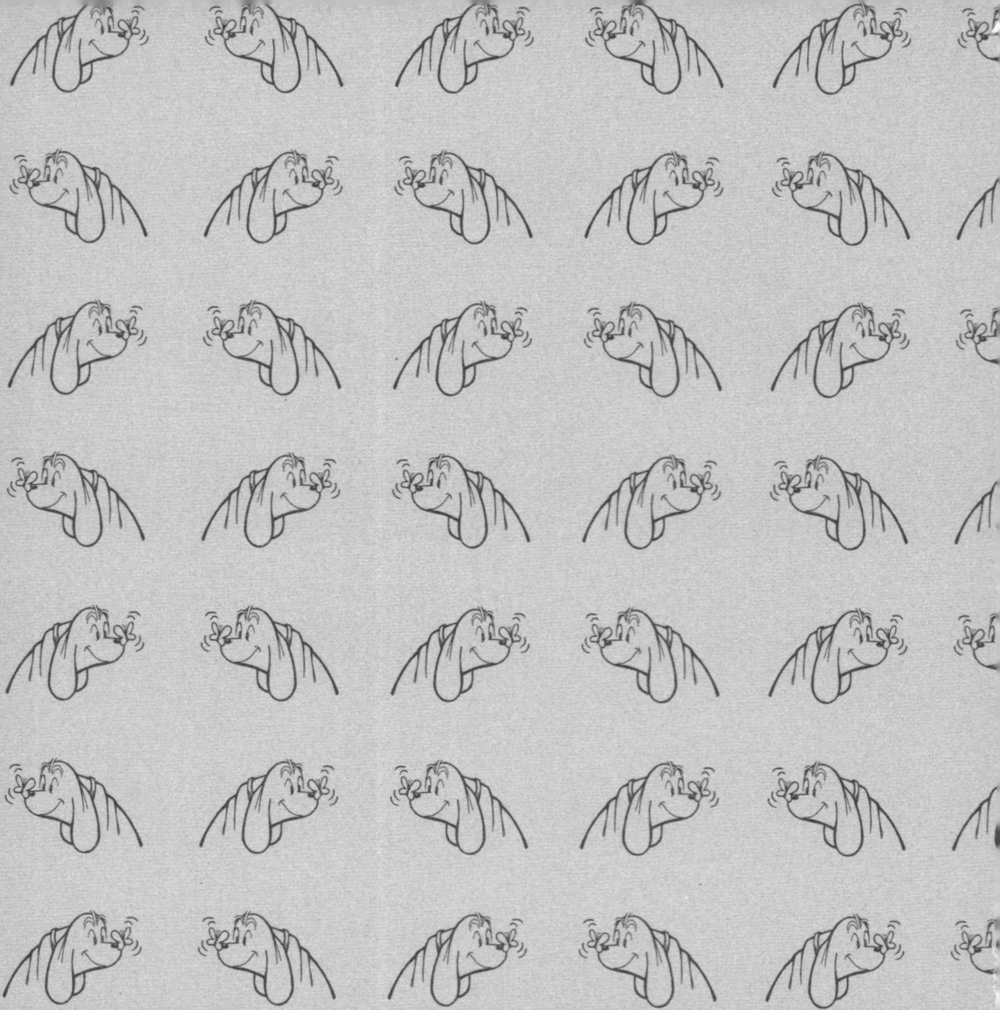